Karen M_____

PUFFIN BOOKS · Ed_____

THE ROAD TO M_____

'Vikings,' said a character in Henry Treece's earlier book, 'are tied to salt-water as a prisoner is tied with chains ! No, there's no understanding them ! They're either madmen – or heroes !'

And Harald Sigurdson is such a one. After his desperate journey to the Hebrides he might be expected to rest in his native land, but he cannot, and when a dark stranger brings to the village news of a fabulous hoard of treasure in Ireland, guarded by the fearsome giant Grummoch, Harald enlists a crew for his longship and sets sail. His quest, and the gruesome battle with Grummoch and the wily king of Murdea, lead to yet stranger adventures. Captured by pirates, then cruelly treated as slaves by Moors, the seafarers, with the now tamed Grummoch, reach at last the towered city of Miklagard, at the very outposts of their world, and there find rich treasure, cruel intrigue, and relentless enemies at the court of the empress Irene. Finally, after bitter hardship, but with the indomitable courage and loyalty to their comrades of the true Viking, they escape and begin the long journey home.

This second book in Henry Treece's magnificent epic of the Viking era, is followed by *Viking's Sunset*, in which Harald makes his last and most perilous voyage.

Cover design by Victor Ambrus

Miklagard   *Illustrated by Christine Price*

Puffin Books in association
with The Bodley Head

Puffin Books, Penguin Books Ltd, Harmondsworth,
Middlesex, England
Penguin Books Australia Ltd, Ringwood,
Victoria, Australia
Penguin Books Canada Ltd,
41 Steelcase Road West,
Markham, Ontario, Canada
Penguin Books (N.Z.) Ltd,
182–190 Wairau Road,
Auckland 10, New Zealand

First published by The Bodley Head 1957
Published in Puffin Books 1967
Reprinted 1972, 1975
Copyright © Henry Treece, 1957

Made and printed in Great Britain by
C. Nicholls & Company Ltd
Set in Linotype Juliana

Contents

PART ONE   1. The Dark Stranger   11

2. The Feast and What Befell There   18

3. The Sailing   30

4. Dun-An-Oir   38

5. The Island Treasure House   49

6. The Bargainers   58

7. The Small Dark Men   67

8. Slave Market   72

PART TWO   9. The House at Jebel Tarik   85

10. What Happened in the Great Courtyard   96

11. The Empty Bed   103

12. The Vengeance of Abu Mazur   109

13. To Sea Again   114

PART THREE   14. Marriba's Command   123

15. The Ship of War   128

16. Miklagard   135

17. The Challenge   140

18. The Mousetrap and What It Caught   149

19. A New Enemy   156

20. Unexpected Ally   167

21. Marriba's End   178

22. City in Flames   186

23. The Inland Sea   197

PART FOUR   24. The Empty Land   205

25. A Surprise by the Fjord   219

HARALD'S ROUTE TO MIKLAGARD AND BACK

KHAZAR KINGDOM

The Great Portage where ships were carried from one river to another

Kiev

Dnieper River

INLAND SEA

MAGYARS

BULGARS

Chrysopolis

Miklagard

EASTERN ROMAN EMPIRE

MIDDLE SEA

NORTHMEN

EMPIRE OF THE FRANKS

Narbo

MOORS

Jebel Tarik

About this Book

In *Viking's Dawn*, I described how a young Northman, Harald Sigurdson, sailed on a voyage with Thorkell Fairhair about the year A.D. 780, and how, after many adventures in Scotland and the Hebrides, he returned home to the village by the fjord, the sole survivor of the ship's company.

The Road to Miklagard is set about five years later, when Harald has grown to be a warrior, respected in his village, and describes how once more he has the urge to 'go a-viking'; but this time his travels take him farther afield – to Ireland, where many Kings still reigned; to Spain, where the victorious Moors had set up their Moslem kingdom; to distant Miklagard, or Constantinople, where the wicked Irene fought to gain power over her weak son, Constantine, so as to rule the Eastern Roman Empire herself; and finally, across the great plains of what is now Russia, and so home again.

On such occasions, many men set out, but few returned. Yet such was the Viking wanderlust that the hazards of their journeys in no way deterred them; indeed, one can imagine that the possible dangers lent attraction to their voyages!

They were a grimly humorous people, who loved nothing better after the voyaging and the fighting were done than to sit at the feast-board and spin their long and sometimes impossible yarns about the places they had been to and the wonders they had seen.

Besides, they were insatiable treasure-hunters; and who would *not* sail half-way round the world if, at the journey's end, there was waiting such wealth as might stagger the imagination to dream of it, even !

To the Northmen, Miklagard was the storehouse of such riches; the magnetic City of Gold. So, it is inevitable that at last Harald Sigurdson must find his face set towards Miklagard.

HENRY TREECE

Part One

Chapter **I** *The Dark Stranger*

The late afternoon sun burned a deep copper-red behind the gaunt hills of the west, slowly sinking to its salty bed among the great grey breakers beyond Ultima Thule, the Last Island, whose silvery beaches of a myriad shells were strewn with the countless wrecks of all the fine longships that had never come back to the fjords. And now they were no longer fine; only grim spars of blackening, salt-encrusted wood, home for the barnacle, playground for the merry barking seals who danced in the secret silver light of the moon, calling to each other in their age-old language, the tongue of those who were familiar with all the rocks in all the seas of all the world – long before man had dared leave his caves to paddle his frightened little shell of a coracle across the width of a meadow stream.

A tall, golden-haired boy sat thinking things as he watched over a herd of swine on a little plateau of green grass, at the edge of a thick beechwood, high up above the dark green waters of the fjord.

'I am Harald Sigurdson,' he said to himself sadly; 'the son of a great sea-rover. Yet I have made only two voyages, and now my dear father is dead and gone to Odin. We shall never sail together again; and all I am fit for is to watch that old Thorn's pigs do not get carried away by a wolf, or eat something which disagrees with them!'

He gave a wry smile of resignation and looked down at

his hands and arms. They were burnt almost black by the
sun, and scarred from finger-tip to elbow. And as he
looked at each scar, he recalled the occasion which had
created it . . .

'This one came when I fought in the torchlight beside
Bjorn, in the long-house in Pictland, when they betrayed
us while we slept. Poor Bjorn, rest in Valhalla . . . And
this one came when I tried to drag the rocks off great
Aun Doorback, as we escaped from Leire's dungeon. May
Aun be happy in Valhalla with his comrade, Gnorre
Nithing . . . I almost wish I were with them, to hear the
tales they will tell . . . And this scar came when I strug-
gled with the sinking currach, far off the coast of
Caledonia, with John the Priest supporting me until the
Danish longship found me . . .'

Harald Sigurdson passed his hand over his eyes and
said, 'Dear John, we shall never see your like again. The
priests who have come here are not of your mettle, good
friend. They think more of words than deeds. Alas, that
I shall never see you again. Your heaven is not my own.'

He glanced over his shoulder, down the steep hill, to
where the village lay, snuggling along the shore of the
great fjord. The blue wood smoke was twisting now as the
sun set. They would be laying the tables with barley
bread and a roast pig, filling the drinking-horns with
honey mead and heather ale; all for the feast.

Harald must be there, he knew, for he was the shipmaster of the village by the fjord, after his experiences
a-viking, adventures which no other man in the place
could equal. Yet his heart was heavy.

'My father should be the shipmaster,' he said to himself. 'I am not worthy to step into his shoes. But he is gone, gone after only one voyage with me ...'

Bitterly he recalled the one foray they had made on a sleepy little coastal village in Northumbria. The northmen had been confident that all would be well, that they would return to their ship with bags of barley meal and baskets of eggs. Then Sigurd had been struck down by an arrow that flew out of the darkness, and the others had turned to find their longship ablaze ... They had sailed, empty-handed, carrying their dead leader, in a ship that more resembled a funeral pyre than a vessel. Harald remembered how they had wallowed off-shore, trying to put out the blaze with their cloaks, with salt water from their helmets, even by rolling on the flames, stifling them with their own bodies.

It had been a sad homecoming for them, for that ship had cost the villagers three years of harvest to buy. Old Thorn, the Headman, had been furious, waving his stick and spluttering all manner of curses on the weary vikings who dragged the charred hulk ashore.

Yet even Thorn had let fall a tear when they carried the body of Sigurd up the runway, back to his lonely hut, for of all men, old Thorn most loved and respected Sigurd, the noble warrior who had chosen to make his home in the sprawling wattle-and-daub village by the fjord.

And now Sigurd's only son, Harald, sat mourning for his father at sunset, among the grubbing swine at the edge of the high beechwoods.

But at last he rose and fastened the hide-strapping round his breeches, getting ready to go down to the feast.

'Only the bear's widow mourns for more than one day,'

he said, recalling an old Norse saying. 'And she soon gets caught!'

He was about to lay his stick on the back of an old pig that would not herd with the others and come down the hill, when he heard a sudden quick movement among the bushes just within the wood. He waited for a moment, expecting to see a fox or a badger, but when nothing appeared, he forgot the noise and turned once more towards the little path that spidered its way downwards to the thatched roofs of the village.

And at that moment, a man ran out from the beech-woods, swift as an attacking wolf, and kicking Harald's feet from under him, sat astride the boy, his knees pinning Harald's arms. The pigs grunted and stopped once more, searching for something else to eat among the heather-covered rocks. The man above Harald snarled, 'If you shout I shall kill you. Believe me, I am a hungry man. I set no store by the laws of this place.'

Harald did his best to smile up at him and said, 'By your black hair and the sort of brooch you wear, I judge you to be a Dane. We have a saying in my village: "Trust a snake before a Frank, a Frank before an Englishman – but do not trust a Dane at all!"'

The man grinned down with fury and said, 'It is true. I am a Dane, and I am proud to be such. But that is neither here nor there. I am a hungry man at this moment, and I swear by my gods and yours that I will let nothing stand between me and my hunger. I want only one of your pigs, a small one will do. But I cannot carry it whole into the forest. I shall kill it and carve it here. So lie still, for I intend only to give you such a knock on the head as will keep you quiet until I have done what needs to be done.'

He leaned over and took up a round stone that lay by them. Harald tried to move, but was powerless under the great weight on his chest. So he smiled again, as the man raised his hand, and said, 'My friend, why should you knock me on the head, when I can help you? I thought you Danes were better bargainers than that.'

The Dane said, 'Why should you help me to steal your swine? That does not sound likely, coming from a Norseman! No, I must knock you on the head, my friend. You are too strongly built for me to take any chances.'

He raised the stone once more, taking aim. But Harald looked up into his dark eyes with his own sky-blue ones and smiling still, said, 'Very well, what must be, must be; but let me tell you before you go to all this trouble that I would willingly give you a fat pig, and help you to skin and carve it. They are not my pigs, and the man to whom they belong is no special friend of mine.'

Slowly the Dane let fall the stone and got up from Harald's chest. He looked very tired, and Harald observed that a trickle of blood had run from a wound in his shoulder and had dried on his arm. In spite of his rich clothes and his gold-studded belt, he looked like a man who was near the end of his tether.

He stood watching the boy suspiciously. 'You must go before me,' he said 'Choose me a good pig and do what needs to be done. If you try to trick me, I shall ...'

But even as he said that, Harald's leg shot out, striking the Dane at the side of the knee. He staggered, with a hoarse cry, but before he could regain his balance, the boy had slipped sideways and had flung him face-down-wards on to the springy turf.

'Now,' said Harald, drawing the man's arms behind him as he sat astride the Dane, 'who shall be knocked on the head, my friend?'

The Dane said, 'I am a fool, and I deserve to die for trusting the word of a Norseman. Kill me and I shall be satisfied.'

But Harald said suddenly, 'Why should I kill you? You look like a warrior to me, and it would ill-become a swineherd to kill a warrior with a stone. No, instead, I will offer you friendship. You shall come down to the village with me and eat your pig there. What do you say to that?'

For a while the man did not speak. Then at last he said, 'No, I would rather be killed by a swineherd than let any gap-toothed villagers jeer at me for being caught so easily.'

In reply, Harald got off the man's back and stood away from him, his hands open, palms upward, to show that he carried no weapon, not even a stone.

'I am no boaster,' he said. 'I would not say that I had caught you by a trick. But later, when you have fed, if you still wish to die, I will borrow a sword from someone and will do what you ask, decently, in the proper manner.'

Then he took up his stick, and ignoring the Dane, gathered his pigs together into a neat herd, and started off with them down the hill.

When he had gone twenty paces, he heard a cry behind him.

'Wait,' shouted the Dane. 'I will come with you. We can talk about swords when I have a meal inside me.'

Harald nodded and said, 'That is just what I told you, my friend.' He handed the staff to the Dane.

'I see you are limping, my friend. Lean on this. I can drive the pigs on with a smack of the hand.'

The Dane took the staff, wondering. Then he smiled and said, 'Judging by the size of your hands, my friend, I wager the pigs would rather be struck with your staff!'

So, laughing, they reached the village.

Old Thorn was beside himself with rage when he saw the guest he was to entertain. Though half-crippled with rheumatism, he bobbed up and down in his anger on the hide-thong bed where he usually lay, and threatened Harald with his stick, saying that the village had little enough for itself, without giving entertainment to good-for-nothing Danes, who ate up all they could, then brought their families in longships the next year to pillage their hosts.

As he raved in the smoke-filled hut, the Dane shuffled his feet with irritation; but Harald still smiled as he laid his hand on the man's shoulder.

'Send him away, and send me, Thorn,' he said softly. 'My father would have counselled you as I do. My father, Sigurd, would not have forgotten the laws of hospitality.'

Thorn's eyes goggled and a vein stood out in his thin neck. But at last he was quiet again and said, 'Be it as you say. He shall stay as long as he wishes. But mark me, he has the look of a pursued man about him, and that bodes no good to anyone. What if he is a nithing, then? What if his king sends for him, and takes our heads too?'

The Dane said, 'I am no nithing, old man. As for my king, he is dead and will never send here for me. He was my brother, and I should have ruled in his place, but for my taste for sailing the seas in longships.'

When Thorn heard that their visitor was of royal blood, he put a rein on his temper and even tried to smile.

'Well, well,' he said, 'then you still may be useful to us. Though you have indeed a look about you which I have seen on the faces of men who are pursued.'

The Dane said, 'We are all pursued, old man; and the one who pursues us will get us, each one of us, in the end.'

Old Thorn, who was very superstitious, crossed his fingers at those words, to keep away Loki, the evil spirit, who listened at the chimney hole to what men said.

Harald laughed and said, 'So, you have been a-viking, Dane! What sights did you see?'

The Dane snorted and replied, 'Such sights as may not be told, young fellow, for fear of keeping sleep from a boy's eyes for a year or more!'

Harald answered, 'I could match them, Dane.'

But the Dane had turned and was looking across the village compound, up towards the hills again, listening, as though he expected someone to come leaping down the heather-covered rocks towards the houses.

Then the horn sounded to summon the villagers to the feast in the long-hall.

Soon the oaken table was thronged about with men and women, for this was not a warrior-meeting, where only the men gathered; and soon the long pinewood hall was thick with smoke from the wood fire in the centre, so that one could hardly see from one side to the other. The village folk ate their pork and barley bread ravenously, each trying to outdo his neighbour and to get good value from the occasion, for each had contributed his share. Then, when the mead-horn had passed round the board a time or two, and the heather ale had been poured into the great helmet and sampled by all, men began to cry out for a song.

The village sagaman, old Nessi, so old that he had to be carried in his chair by two boys wherever he went, began to strike on a little drum with the flat of his dry old hand, giving himself a rhythm to work to. His drum was an earthen gourd, covered by a tight and thinly-scraped sheepskin, bound about with deer sinews. It gave off a sharp little note that cut through the talk about the table and caused all the villagers, even the most quick-tongued woman, to fall silent, while the bard declaimed his words.

> 'There are three things a man should fear,
> A wolf, a sword, and a woman.'

He sang, smiling wickedly.

The men began to laugh and the women to make angry faces at the old poet. But when the uproar had died again, he started again more seriously and sang,

> 'It came from no man knows where;
> It hides beneath the deepest rocks;
> It will not be wooed with promises;
> Yet most men love it better than life itself.
> What say you, wise ones, that it is?'

The hall was filled with the voices of men and women, who tried to guess the answer to the riddle. But at each attempt, the sagaman shook his head and smiled.

Then he looked towards the Dane who sat between Thorn and Harald, at the head of the table.

'You seem to be a quick-witted fellow,' said the bard. 'Will you not try to guess?'

The Dane shrugged his broad shoulders and smiled. 'I shall not need to guess,' he said. 'For I know what the answer is. I made up that song myself, at my brother's house in Hedeby, many years ago. The answer is: *Gold*, nothing more!'

At first there was silence, then there was an excited shouting among the people. The sagaman smiled and said, 'I recognized you, Arkil the Prince, as soon as you came in. That is why I tried your own song on you. Here, take the drum; I hand it to a better bard than myself.'

The people clapped Arkil on the back and made him go forward, against his will, to stand beside the fire and sing them a song. He struck the drum a time or two, but then flung it back to the sagaman, saying, 'I can get along better in my own way, Nessi the Bard'.

And he began to clap his hands against each other, making many different sounds, and many complicated rhythms. The folk in the hall would have been well contented to hear him clapping like that for long enough, but the Dane suddenly began to sing in a deep musical voice:

'Away where the seal plays,
In the light of the dying sun,
Where the wave rocks forever
The white bones of the great sailors,
And the ghosts of all longships
Swing on the tides,
There have I been.

I have been where
The halls of the sunset
Echo with song, echo with voices
Of all the great army
Of those who have left us,
Left us to roam.'

As he stood there, in the flickering firelight, a strange look came over his face. He seemed to be asleep, or voyaging in a dream among the islands of his song. And the folk in the hall gazed at him raptly, sharing his vision.

Then suddenly the door was flung open and a great gust of cold air scattered the ashes of the fire, and brought everyone back to the world they knew, with its harsh chill.

'Who has opened the door?' shouted old Thorn angrily, grabbing his stick to lay it about the shoulders of the man who had been so careless.

But then men gasped. Standing in the doorway were two strange and frightening figures. They were bigger men than anyone at that feast had seen before, bigger even than Aun Doorback himself had been. Their long black hair was knotted up with bone pins, and about their bodies they wore thick corselets of horsehide. Each carried a long, leaf-bladed sword of bronze and the firelight glistened on the broad streaks of blue which stretched across their dark cheeks. They smiled grimly to see the fear they had roused among the villagers.

Then one of them spoke. 'I opened the door, old man,' he said. 'Will you beat me with your little stick, then?'

Old Thorn was a brave man, despite his age and his rheumatism. He began to rise, saying, 'Aye, that I will, whoever you may be!'

But Harald pulled him back on to his seat. 'Take care, Thorn,' he said. 'These are lawless Irishmen; I see that from their coloured breeches, which are such as their inland tribes still wear. Do not anger them.'

When their first shock was over, many men cursed themselves for obeying the old feast laws, which decreed that they must leave their weapons at home; while the women wished they had their ladles or rolling-pins.

One woman, Thora, the niece of Thorn, a strong-armed creature with a great reputation for keeping her husband in order, rose and called out, 'If only I had my skinning-knife, you rascals, I'd make you skip back to Ireland, and glad to go! That I would!'

Then the other Irishman spoke, coldly and viciously, 'If we had the time, woman, we would teach you the lesson your husband should have taught you by now. But we are not concerned with you folk. Our man stands there. We have followed him half over the world and shall not let him go for the threats of a room-full of midden-churls and their women.'

He pointed with his sword at Arkil the Dane, who still stood by the fire, the sagaman's drum by his side on the table.

Arkil shrugged his shoulders, 'You have come a long way to find me. Now let us go outside and settle this quarrel properly, as men should, without disturbing the feast.'

The Irishmen smiled grimly and shook their heads.

'What we have to do shall be done here, without delay,' said the first one. 'We cannot risk losing you in the darkness again.'

They saw that Arkil was trapped, with his back against the table, and they saw also that he carried no sword or axe. They moved across the space towards him, their blades raised to strike. The horrified men and women about the tables saw that the Dane still smiled, and made no attempt to run from the threatened blows.

Yet as the first great Irishman struck downwards with his sword, the Dane flung the sagaman's drum at him with all his force. The earthen jar shattered to pieces with the impact, and the Irishman staggered backwards, with a cry of pain, his hands to his face.

Then there was a great shout from the head of the table and Harald leapt forward, scattering dishes before him in his haste. He could not reach the second Irishman in time to grapple with him, but did something even more terrible. As he passed the fireplace, he snatched up a flaming log and flung it at the barbaric figure. The Irishman swung round, trying to ward off the brand with his sword, and in that moment, Arkil leapt upon his back, bearing him down.

Men rushed from the nearest end of the table now, anxious to attack the first Irishman, who had recovered from the blow he had received from the drum; but they were too late. Harald had kicked the half-blinded man's feet from under him and was sitting astride his back, his fingers deep in the man's black hair, banging his head rhythmically on the hard earthen floor.

Soon Arkil rose, smiling strangely, the sword of his opponent in his hand.

He said simply, 'That one will not spoil a feast again. Now let me take his brother outside, Harald, my friend.

He shall have better treatment than he would have allowed me. He shall take his sword with him into the darkness.'

No man, not even Thorn, could deny Arkil his right in this matter. And shortly the Dane came back into the hall, carrying two swords this time, and smiling as one who could now get on with his supper without fear of interruption.

But first he flung the two swords on to the sheepskins beside the walls, saying, 'The village boys will play happily with these. They are of no worth. I doubt whether a man could cut himself with them if he tried!'

And to the sagaman he said, 'One day, my friend, I will repay you a golden harp for that drum, for it saved my life this night'.

Then he stood near Harald and took him by both hands. 'May the seas have me and the crows eat my heart if I am ever false to you, my friend,' he said, in the time-honoured oath.

And when he sat down again, he put his hand inside his tunic and drew out two things; a long package and a round one. When he had unwrapped the deerskin from the long package, the villagers saw that it was a knife of gold, its hilt carved and moulded so beautifully that all the women gasped with envy; its blade chased from end to end with fine runes, which glistened in the torch-light.

The round package, he opened more carefully, and then let fall a glittering cascade of coloured stones on to the table, where they lay, glinting beautifully as the light from the wall-torches touched them. Now all men rose to their feet in astonishment, and Arkil smiled and gathered his treasure once more into the bag.

To Thorn he said, 'You were right, headman, I was pursued; but I am pursued no longer. Those who came after me to regain their giant's treasure are no more.'

Thorn said, 'You have stolen a giant's treasure, have you! And an Irish giant at that! Well, and what do you mean to do now, Arkil the Prince?'

The Dane smiled and said, 'I propose to gather a shipful of fighting-cocks about me and to go back and steal the rest of his treasure, for this is but a tiny drop in the ocean.'

Thorn's eyes gleamed as red and green as the jewels themselves with greed. He said, 'My step-brother, Alaf, who farms higher up the fjord, has a good ship, which he is a little too old to sail in now. I have no doubt that I could persuade him to sell it to you for that bag of pretty stones.'

The Dane smiled slowly and then said, 'This bag of pretty stones, as you call them, would buy a ship made of gold with sails of silk, old man. Nay, nay, I will buy your step-brother's ship with three of my pretty stones at the most – not a grain of dust more!'

Thorn's face showed his annoyance and for a moment it looked as though he might quarrel with Arkil the Prince; but he saw the reason in what the Dane said, for after all, this man had risked his life to gain those precious stones, and the boat was worth no more than Arkil said.

But Thorn was not a man to be beaten in a bargain.

'Look you, Prince,' he said at last, 'buy my step-brother's

ship, and I will provide her with a stout crew from the men of my village.'

The Dane screwed up his eyes, amused now. Then he nodded.

'That seems a good plan, headman,' he said, 'for I have seen that your village breeds good men. But what price must I pay for their service? I cannot imagine that you offer them for the love of it.'

Thorn's long forefinger drew a little pattern on the oaken table-top as he spoke. 'I shall ask two-thirds of whatever treasure you shall bring back, to be given to the village. For after all, it has not done badly by you in your need.'

Arkil clapped the old man on the shoulder.

'By Odin,' he said, 'when I next go to market to buy a cow, I shall take you with me, old man. There is not a better bargainer in the northern lands than you. Well, I agree to what you ask, for if we find the treasure I have mentioned, one third of it will satisfy me – and will keep me in comfort for the rest of my days.'

So they shook hands on the bargain, and the next day Arkil and Harald went with Thorn to Alaf's steading, higher up the fjord. Alaf accepted the price the Dane offered without any argument, for he was not a shrewd haggler as Thorn was.

Alaf's longship lay in the cow-byre, where it had been dragged when he gave up voyaging five years before. It was a well-built boat, but a bit heavy, the Dane said, for the rivers it would sail up in Ireland. He would have preferred a ship broader in the belly and sitting lower in the water.

'But beggars cannot be choosers,' said Thorn, 'and I am setting you up with a crew straightaway; you will have no seeking to do.'

The Dane looked at him through narrowed lids.

'My friend,' he said, 'with my knowledge of the treasure, and my reputation in my own land, I could fit out fifty little ships like this, at one whistle.'

Then, seeing Thorn's crestfallen expression, he touched him on the arm and went on, 'But I should find no better men than those of yours if I went whistling along every fjord in the northland.'

So they paid for the longship, which Arkil named *Seeker*, and the next day twenty men dragged her on rollers down to the village.

Chapter 3 The Sailing

Arkil found no difficulty in getting together his crew. The real difficulty lay in picking twenty out of the hundred men who jostled round the table, anxious to sail with him. Harald sat with Arkil at the table, for the boy was named shipmaster without any argument, while Arkil held himself merely to be the leader once they were ashore in Ireland.

So, just as Thorkell Fairhair had done, five years before on that very spot, Harald gave the new crew the knuckle bones, as symbols that they were signed on as crew members in the *Seeker*. And each man, as he took the bones, gave his solemn promise to obey orders and to fight for his comrades, whatever the odds.

Many good men came up to the table that day, laying their weapons before their new masters and naming them as they took the oath. There was Haro 'Once-only', with his sword, *Alas*; Sven Hawknose, with his axe, *Sweetheart*; Elf Elfson, with his axe, *Trouble-me-no-more*; Kran the Lark, a great singer, with his dagger, *Forget-me-not*; Jago Longarm, with his axe, *Wife's Lament*; Skirr Barrel a great drinker, with his mace, *Thunderstone*; and many more. Harald had his long sword, which had belonged to his father once. It was called *Sigurd's Darling*, and had a curiously carved hilt of walrus ivory which was the envy of all who saw it. As for Arkil, his only weapon was the golden knife, which he called *Heart's Desire*. He refused to accept any offer of a weapon, for, as he said, when he needed a weapon, one always seemed to come to hand, whether it was a drum or a log out of the fire. And such weapons did not need cleaning and oiling as swords did!

There was only one mishap before they sailed. It happened when they were stepping the mast. A sudden gust of wind swung the loose pole sideways, pinning Skirr Barrel against the gunwales and breaking his arm. But he took the event with all good humour, and said that in any case he had three casks of heather ale to finish up before it went off, so he did not mind, provided that they took his cousin, Radbard Crookleg, with them in his place.

Arkil the Prince did not care for the look of this Radbard, whose red beard gave him a shifty expression, and whose badly set leg caused him to walk with a slight limp.

But Harald accepted Radbard gladly, for he knew the man to be a true sailor and a brave warrior. As it happened, this Radbard was a lucky choice, and when he looked back on the affair, Harald was compelled to think that the gods who had sent the sudden puff of wind to pin Skirr Barrel down had acted well.

So, when she was laden with dried meats, barley flour, five kegs of water and three of heather ale, all stowed beneath the deck, *Seeker* pulled away from the village, and at last came into the open sea.

The men soon settled down to their new life and the voyage was an uneventful one, save for the occasion when they tried to board a tall ship, which wallowed clumsily off the Anglian coast.

Then, to their cost, the vikings found that the vessel was full of archers on their way to Frankland. Elf Elfson and three others were lost in that affair, though they took more than their own number with them to Valhalla.

After that, both Harald and Arkil took a turn at the oars. And on the fifth day out, just when their water was finished, they sighted the port of Murdea, which Arkil told them was the nearest point to the kingdom they were making for.

It was a squalid looking harbour, with wooden houses seeming to hang above the water, supported on piles which were gradually rotting, to let their loads heel slowly over into the dark and rubbish-littered tide. Over the township, which was set on a low hill, a heavy cloud of smoke hung perpetually, as the grey sea-birds flew in and out of it, crying discordantly.

Kran the Lark blew his nose lustily and said aloud, 'Even a blind man would know when he had reached Murdea!'

Sven Hawknose tugged at his long yellow moustaches and said quietly, 'Could a blind man find his way back home *from* Murdea, think you, Kran?'

Then there was silence on board *Seeker*, for they had all heard of the cruelties practised on vikings who were unfortunate enough to get themselves captured in the townships they sacked.

But Arkil cheered them up by saying, 'You need have no fear here, my sea-cocks! I know the headman of Murdea as well as I know most of you – better, if the truth be told!'

'That isn't saying much,' said Haro Once-only, grinning, 'for we are a simple lot. We must be, or we shouldn't be here now!'

When they had furled the sail and rowed to their anchorage, they climbed ashore, up the dangling rope-ladder, leaving Jago Longarm and another viking to guard *Seeker* till they returned.

'Have no dealings with the townsfolk,' warned Arkil as they left. 'Give them no offence and they will not harm you.'

Jago grinned up at him and touched his sword-hilt lightly.

'Have no fear, chieftain,' he said. 'The ship will be here when you want it again.'

The vikings walked in a body up the winding street, followed by a group of hangers-on and children, who admired their helmets and their various weapons, noisily and with many gestures.

Sven Hawknose flung a coin to one of the raggedest of their followers. He picked it up and then spat on it, before flinging it back at Sven's feet.

'Now you know,' said Harald, laughing, 'Keep your money in your pouch, Sven; it is a bad bargain to throw it into the gutter without even getting thanks for it.'

Sven muttered angrily and said that if he could lay his hands on that ragged rogue, he would cut his hair for him – with an axe.

The headman of Murdea greeted them at his tumble-down door, but the look on his face was one of annoyance rather than pleasure. And when they were all inside, he said hurriedly, 'My friends, things are not now as they once were here. The vikings have made a bad name for themselves, and the folk of the town say they will stand it no longer. I who am half a viking, my father having been a Dane, think that it is stupidity, but my wife, who is Irish, sides with them and says that the northmen are a curse from God for our misdeeds in the past. Whatever is the truth, I do not know; but all I can tell you is to go away from Murdea with the next tide.'

Arkil thanked him for his advice and then bought wine from him. They all sat together on the floor and drank from the few cups that the headman possessed, passing the vessels from one to the other.

Harald noticed that the headman himself refused the wine, saying that he was suffering from a chill on the stomach and could not appreciate it. Harald spoke about this to Arkil, saying, 'It is a bad sign when a man will not drink his own wine. I have heard of travellers being poisoned by that trick before now. The headman must drink his own wine, then we shall be sure that he has dealt with us in good faith.'

So Radbard held the man still while Harald poured a cup of the tart wine down his throat. The man protested and spluttered a great deal, but did not fall dead; and so the vikings were satisfied.

Then suddenly the guard they had put on the street door, Goff Goffling, ran in and shouted out, 'Come quickly, my masters, there is such a light shining down at the harbour as can mean only one thing!'

The vikings raced down the rough street, Harald and

Arkil in the lead, full of foreboding. Their fears were realized, when they turned a corner and saw the *Seeker* a mass of fire, down to the water-line, and already foundering.

They found Jago Longarm lying with his head dangling over the edge of the harbour jetty, a great wound in his back. He smiled up at them as they lifted him up and said, 'Four of them will greet their gods tonight, master. But I am sorry about the ship.'

Then he died without speaking again. As the *Seeker* slowly settled down in the water, the body of the other viking guard floated up to the surface for a moment.

All men saw the colour of his tunic and recognized it. Then he went down in the suction of the sinking ship.

Haro Once-only turned towards the town, pulling at his moustaches and cursing horribly. He was a notorious berserk and had to be kept under control when any trouble started, or he was inclined to rip off his shirt and run screaming at the enemy, dealing dreadful slaughter. It was a madness that ran in his family, for his six brothers had also been berserks, though they had not lasted as long as Haro, who had never received a wound in more than fifty affrays and five voyages.

Arkil went up to him and said softly, 'Patience, friend Haro. I too am of the same turn of mind. My own shirt will seldom stay on my body once I feel the little hairs prickling at the top of my neck. But patience, we must wait. One day we will burn this rat's nest out, and then our two will be avenged.'

Now they had no ship and no food, and a hostile township before them. Arkil turned away from the harbour suddenly and strode towards the biggest house he could see. The others followed him. It was the house of a rich merchant, it turned out, and soon the vikings had broken open two sacks of meal and had filled their flasks with clear grape wine.

'At least we shall not starve for two days,' said Arkil, 'and that is all we need if I can find my way through the bogs again.'

As they left the silent house, a shower of arrows came at them from the other side of the street. No one was hurt, but Harald felt one shaft pass between his arm and his body, and afterwards saw it still quivering in the door he had just passed through.

'That is a good omen,' said Arkil, 'and, it seems to me, we shall need all the luck we can get.'

Then, led by Kran, whose voice sounded out over the town like a great bell, the vikings sang their war-song as they marched up the narrow winding street to the top of the town. No further harm came to them, though they often saw men run round corners, or draw back from windows as they passed, and not one of the crew but expected to feel an arrow shaft in his back a moment later.

At the top of the hill stood a little white church, with a small square tower. Haro was all for going inside and sacking it, but Harald took him by the arm and said, 'But for one of those men who follow the Christ, I should not be here today. If you lay a hand on the Christman's belongings, you will have me for an enemy, my friend. And I should not like that, Haro.'

Haro grinned and punched Harald in the chest. 'No, nor should I,' he said. And so they passed over the hill without burning that church.

As for the vikings, they were not so happy after an hour's walking, for the memory of their lost comrades had come back to them, and made them wonder whether the treasure they had come to seek was not guarded by ill-fortune. Besides, they had now begun to strike the marshy land, where habitations were few and far between and the roads had almost ceased to exist.

But Arkil strode on purposefully, giving no hint of the doubt that had already come into his own mind.

Chapter 4 *Dun-An-Oir*

On the third day after their retreat from Murdea, the vikings lay down, exhausted, in a little green gully that gave them some slight shelter from the night wind. Their clothes hung in shreds and each man was filthy with mud from the waist down.

Now their minds were filled with nothing but the thought of that everlastingly green countryside, where the ground gave suddenly beneath one's feet, to leave one floundering in the choking slime.

'We cannot go on much farther, Arkil,' said Harald himself. 'I have known many hardships, but this is the worst; yes, even worse than the flogging-post at Leire's Dun.'

Arkil licked his dry lips; 'Have courage, Harald boy,' he said. 'We have not much farther to go, if my reckoning is right. There is a great blue hill, shaped like a cow's back, with hawthorns growing the length of it. And on the other side of that lies Dun-an-oir, the Fort of Gold. That is our journey's end.'

Haro Once-only said sharply, 'You should not use such words, Arkil the Prince. Odin might make it your journey's end in all faith.'

Arkil said, 'I am weary, Haro my friend. Do not tease me or I might hit you with my fist, and then you would fall into such a dreamland that even you would not care what Odin thought!'

Haro shrugged his shoulders and said, 'I wish you

would, for I am dying slowly of hunger and thirst. Two cupfuls of porridge is no food for a grown man like me to live on for three days.'

Arkil said, 'Tomorrow you will feast on sweet sheep-meat and the crispest of rye bread. Have patience.'

Then, to keep the men's minds from hunger and thirst and cold, Arkil said, 'There is not a poet among you all, save myself. Listen, I will tell you a verse I have just made:

'The white shears cut the green,
But the shears are not of iron
Nor the green of grass.'

Sven Hawknose said, 'That is an easy one. I have known children make better riddles. That is a seagull skimming over the sea.'

Arkil said, 'You are right, Sven. But can you make one which I could not guess?'

Sven said, 'Yes, I give you this one:

'This shining snake has no home
And so must make one in the white rock;
But it is chased away by the red river
And can rest nowhere.'

Arkil said, 'You are clever, but not clever enough, old friend. That is a sword making a wound.'

Then Harald said, 'You both rhyme like young girls in the bower. Let me tell you one, and if you guess this, I will let each one of you give me a kick:

'When we have you not
We want you;
But when we have you
We do not know.'

The vikings sat and scratched their heads, making many guesses, but not one of them right. Then, when they had given up, Harald said, 'It is sleep; and that is what I am going to have now.'

So without another word he wrapped his tattered cloak about him and, snuggling close against the side of the gully, he fell into a doze, which at least kept his mind from thoughts of food and drink. The others followed suit, tired by their long march, and when the sun rose again, they set off towards the west and, after much floundering in the marshland, rested once more on the peak of a little hill.

It was then that Goff Goffling ran back to Arkil, saying that he had seen two wonderful things; to the west he had suddenly glimpsed the hill shaped like a cow's back; and below the hill they were on, he had seen a herd of horses, with only one man to guard them.

This news cheered the wanderers immensely, and Arkil and Harald crept quietly to their hill's edge to test Goff's words. True enough, in the morning haze they saw the great hill shaped like a cow's back, beyond which lay the Fort of Gold, their destination; and below them, a great herd of horses grazed, guarded by a tired-looking horseman, his black hair held up by pins, his legs encased in coloured breeches. Arkil noted that the man carried a long bronze sword and a cruel-looking lance.

'The important thing is not to give him time to use them,' said Harald, 'for he looks like a warrior who would sell his life dearly to protect such fine beasts.'

Arkil nodded and whispered, 'Is there anyone among us who can throw a stone, young friend?'

Harald nodded and said, 'Radbard Crookleg can hit a sparrow with an acorn at twenty paces.'

So they signalled back to Radbard, who found himself three good-sized flints and then began to creep down the hillside towards the horseman. The vikings watched him go, holding their breath with anxiety.

The horseman's back was towards them, and men soon began to chuckle as Radbard drew nearer and nearer. Then something happened which put their hearts in their mouths, for suddenly the great black stallion on which the man sat raised his fierce head and gave a high warning neigh. Immediately the herd swung round, stopping their grazing, snorting and whinnying. Radbard stood up then and threw with all his might. But the stallion had seen him and reared in anger. The stone missed the rudely awakened rider, but struck the horse on the neck.

With a high bound, the startled animal swung round, flinging its rider down, and for an instant all was panic among the great herd.

Then Arkil was on his feet. 'Run, run,' he shouted, 'before the man is up again!'

And like a ragged army, the sixteen wanderers streamed down the hill towards the swirling horses, each man grasping the mane of the creature nearest to him.

The guard had been kicked on the shoulder and sat ruefully rubbing his arm as Harald came up with him. He glared ferociously at the boy, but brightened up when he saw Arkil, who knelt down beside him and shook him by the hand. 'Why, Saidhe, old friend,' he said, 'and to think that I did not recognize you!'

The Irishman grinned painfully and said, 'Arkil the

Prince, and to think that you dare come back here after what giant Grummoch vowed to do to you! But it is good to see you again, and I can tell you that King MacMiorog will not turn you away this time, especially as you bring such fine men to fight for him.'

Arkil said, 'That is as may be, Saidhe! But our quest is for our own good, not King MacMiorog's. Where is giant Grummoch at the moment, my friend?'

Saidhe rose from the ground and whistled his black horse back to him; the half-savage creature snorted violently at the nearness of the vikings, but his master whispered something to him, and he became calm once more.

Then Saidhe replied, 'You are in luck. Giant Grummoch is away in the north, at the court of the High King, asking the hand of his beautiful daughter. So you will be able to talk to King MacMiorog without interruption for a while.'

And so it was that the vikings rode over the hill shaped like a cow's back and saw for the first time Dun-an-oir, the Fort of Gold.

To many of them, this was the most splendid place they had ever seen, and they began to say that neither Kiev nor Byzantium itself could be as wonderful, though of course they had not seen either.

Dun-an-oir lay golden in the morning sunshine, surrounded by a high stockade, a place of many fine houses, with the wood-smoke curling up blue above the thatched roofs.

Goff Goffling groaned and pointed to the many heads which nodded on tall pikes the length of the stockade wall.

'You treat your visitors badly,' he said to Saidhe.

Saidhe grinned and said, 'There is not a viking head among them all, my friend. King MacMiorog is a good Christian and would not decorate his city with the heads of heathens.'

Harald was less concerned with the heads than with the vast herds of black cattle which grazed quietly here and there across the broad plain.

'Indeed, King MacMiorog must be the richest king in Ireland,' he said enviously.

But Saidhe once more shook his black head until the bone pins in his hair began to jingle.

'Nay, nay, young friend,' he said. 'He might be if Giant Grummoch were not here. MacMiorog owns only that which Grummoch will let him own; for he is like a carrion crow who feeds on the best meat himself and leaves little enough behind for the lesser birds to pick.'

Harald said, 'Why does your king allow this giant to go on living off him? Could he not arrange for the giant to join his fathers in whatever heaven giants go to?'

Saidhe shrugged his shoulders, though it seemed to hurt him to do so after his fall, and said, 'MacMiorog was born a coward. He is a strong fighter when his opponent is afraid; but his courage fails him when he meets opposition. The warriors of Dun-an-oir hold him in some contempt and will not attack Grummoch for such a king. So Grummoch rules the roost and makes a good thing out of it, while MacMiorog sits biting his finger-nails in his palace, dreaming of the day when the gods will snatch Grummoch away.' He paused a while and then added, 'But so far the gods seem to prefer Grummoch to remain down here on earth with MacMiorog. His reputation seems to have gone before him to heaven!'

At last they came to the stockade gates, which opened to them after Saidhe had blown three blasts on the horn which hung beside the lintels.

The herd of horses galloped first through the stockade and turned off into a protected paddock within the city, led by the black stallion. Haro Once-only turned longing eyes after them.

'Alas,' he said, 'we might have done well to keep a firm hold on those beasts, for we may need them sooner than we think.'

Saidhe said grimly, 'If things go well with you, the King will give you horses to ride on. But if they go badly, you will not need horses again.'

While the men were wondering about this, Saidhe led them to a long house of timber and thatch, the broad door of which was adorned with seven white skulls, nailed to the timbers with iron spikes. He pointed at the skull in

the centre and said, 'This one came from Orkney to put
an end to Grummoch, but the crows had him within five
days.'

Then they passed by the guard, who lolled against the
doorpost, leaning on his spear, and so into the great hall
itself, where the King sat on a painted throne, made more
comfortable by coverings of sheepskin.

MacMiorog stared at them through the smoke of his
hall and spoke to a little man, dressed in black, who sat on
the floor beside him.

The vikings heard him say, 'Here, Cormac, are the men
you promised me in your dream, the Lochlannoch, men of
the waters. Mayhap they will put a swift end to our
troubles, then we shall sleep soft o' nights once more.'

The King was a bent and wizened creature, a young
man grown old before his time. His thin black beard and
moustaches gave an air of weakness to his pale face, and
even his narrow crown of beaten Irish gold sat crookedly
and comically upon his head. He flung back his shawl of

red and green wool and beckoned to Arkil, who had stepped up before the throne.

'I am glad to see you again, Prince Arkil,' he said, in a soft and womanish voice. 'We thought your head might have come back sooner than your body, for Grummoch sent the two fierce brothers after you. Did you not meet them on your way?'

Arkil bowed a little and said equally softly, 'Yes, King MacMiorog, I met them, and drew their teeth for them. Their bodies have long since fed the fishes of the fjord.'

The King pulled at his beard and forced a smile. 'That is good,' he said. 'For if they had brought your head, it would have been no use to me. There is no space on my door for another one, you see. But coming with your whole body, and with such a goodly company of sea-rovers, you may well be of use to me.'

Arkil said, 'You wish us to put an end to giant Grum-moch, is that not it?'

The King nodded, his thin lips smiling cruelly.

'You are still as keen-sighted as ever, Arkil,' he said. 'Let us pray that Grummoch does not draw the shades of night over those eyes.'

Haro Once-only was becoming tired of this talk, for he was a direct man, and he said suddenly, 'The giant who can do that has yet to be born.'

The King turned his gaze on Haro, as though he had never seen such a creature before, but Haro was not a man to be frightened by a look and he stared back, until King MacMiorog had to give him best and look away.

'Every cock can crow loudly enough in the daylight on his own dunghill,' said the little man in black who sat by the throne, 'but how many cocks dare crow at night, when the fox sniffs under the perch?'

Haro stepped forward then and flung his sword *Alas!* at the feet of MacMiorog.

'Before Odin, I will take that giant's head if it is the last thing I do, just to show you that this cock has spurs as well as a singing voice!'

The King pushed the sword away with his foot as though it were a distasteful thing to him, and said, 'Prince Arkil, a true captain keeps his hounds on the leash. See that this dog is muzzled before you bring him before me again.'

At this the vikings in the hall began to shout out, and some of them even drew their swords and daggers, so that the guards at the door prepared for battle there and then, and were not at all happy about their prospects. But Arkil held up his hand for silence and then he said, 'King Mac-Miorog, we have an old saying in the north. It is this: the wolf whose foot is caught in a trap cannot afford to snarl at the hunter. Think on that saying, King, and we will come before you tomorrow and listen to you then.'

He turned to go, but King MacMiorog called him back, smiling now, and said, 'I was only trying to test your mettle, my friend. Now I know that you are men of good heart and so I give you my trust.'

Then he clapped his hands and slave women came forward with horns of mead and platters of sheepmeat and good barley bread. The vikings sat on the rush-covered floor and ate their fill, and when they had finished, the King spoke once more, saying, 'My friends, you shall live to call me a generous master.'

Sven Hawknose called out, his mouth full of meat, 'We have no masters but Arkil and Harald!'

MacMiorog smiled bitterly at him and went on, 'That is so, I used the word merely as a term of friendship towards you. But I will proceed. This land is ravaged by a giant, as you know. I cannot turn my own men against him, for they fear him; and besides that, I must confess that they do not love me enough to risk their lives for me. So it will fall on you to rid the land of this plague. And in return, you shall take away with you as much of the giant's treasure as you can carry, each man a sackful.'

Arkil stood up before the king and said, 'If we kill Grummoch, we shall take all his treasure, my friend, have no fear.'

King MacMiorog bit his lip and then said, 'Very well, that is as may be; you have a name for being harsh bargainers, you men of the far north. Let it be at that.'

But Harald was not satisfied, for he did not trust this black-haired king with the crooked crown. He rose and went forward, saying, 'Take my hands, King, and swear by your God that you will give us leave to take all the giant's treasure.'

King MacMiorog glowered at Harald, who was only a boy in his eyes, and said, 'I will swear to Prince Arkil, but not to you.'

But Arkil said stoutly, 'Swear to Harald or not at all, for he and I are as two brothers in this matter.'

So King MacMiorog took the oath, holding Harald's hands, and then he promised that he would show them where the treasure lay, so that there might be no error when the time of trial came.

Chapter 5 *The Island Treasure House*

Three days after their arrival at Dun-an-oir, the vikings lolled before the cave entrance on the little island in the lake, below the hill shaped like a cow's back. They had made their home there since the night King MacMiorog had shown where the giant's treasure lay, and each day some of them rowed back to Dun-an-oir to fetch food and drink for the company.

They sat in the sunshine, wondering when giant Grummoch would return to Dun-an-oir, speculating on the nature of the treasure, and working out ways of transporting it back to the coast when they had won it.

Haro and Goff Goffling were in the middle of a tremendous argument on the matter when Sven, who had climbed the one tree on the little island, shouted out that he could see a wagon train approaching Dun-an-oir across the green plain. He said that there were at least ten wagons and that they were drawn by white oxen. It seemed to his eyes that the giant was riding at the head of the column on a black creature, but he could not tell what the creature was. Arkil, whose eyes were keener than those of a hawk, climbed up the tree beside him and said that the creature was a bull. He also said that the giant seemed even bigger than when last he, Arkil, had been in Dun-an-oir, and that was saying much.

Then there was much excitement among the vikings, for each man wanted to climb the tree and see this giant; but the tree was not strong enough to hold them all, and there was no time for them to take turns in climbing it. They were all sent to their various hiding-places, and Arkil himself rowed the little boat round to the far side of the island so that Grummoch should have no suspicion of their presence.

The waiting was terrible for them all, and the only thing they could do was to lie quietly, chewing on the strips of dried meat which MacMiorog had sent them that day. It was almost sunset before they heard the sound of voices on the far shore, and saw the flare of torches start up as men began to load boats and rafts on the other side.

Arkil passed the message round that they were all to lie still and not to attack until he called out like a sparrow hawk; then they were to fall on the giant in a body and put an end to him as swiftly as could be managed.

It was then that they heard Grummoch's voice for the first time, and so strangely high-pitched was it that Haro laughed aloud. Goff punched him in the mouth for that and a fight would have started there and then, but for Arkil's warning that the two would lose their share of the treasure if they did not quieten down immediately.

Then the vikings heard the sound of oars splashing in the waters of the lake, and saw the flare of torchlight growing nearer and nearer.

And suddenly a big boat drew alongside the small landing-beach and they saw for the first time the giant, Grum-

moch, as he waded ashore, carrying two great sacks on his
shoulders.

Harald, who had once known the massive Aun Doorback, gasped in mute astonishment, for this was a bigger
man than he had ever dreamed of. Grummoch was the
height of a man and a half, and was as broad across the
shoulders as three men standing together. The slaves who
came after him, carrying their loads, had almost to run in
order to keep up with his monstrous strides.

From the corner of his eye, Harald saw Arkil wipe the
sweat from his forehead, in anticipation of the fight that
must surely follow the arrival of such an opponent.

Then Harald had a closer view of Grummoch, in the
light of the many torches. His red hair hung in two great
plaits, down each side of his head, and was braided with
strands of gold wire. His thick red ears carried rings in
the shape of half-moons. His massive arms were laden
with bracelets of gold, twisted in spirals; and his fingers
glimmered in the light from the many rings which encircled them. From head to foot, this giant was a treasure-
house in himself. His rich red tunic was embroidered with
silver and gold; rubies and emeralds gleamed on his em-
bossed belt; his sword scabbard flashed with the fire of
many amethysts; even the strappings about his gigantic
thighs were thickly garnished with studs of coral.

As Harald saw the ease with which Grummoch rolled
away the great boulder at the mouth of the treasure cave,
his heart fell, for he and many others had tried for days
to roll away that stone, without success.

Their plan had been that they were to attack when
Grummoch had entered the cave, and before his slaves

could reach him, for it was thought that in the restricted space of the entrance the giant would have less chance of using his great strength on the vikings.

And then Arkil gave the cry of the sparrow hawk, and all men saw him break cover and run shouting towards the cave, Harald close on his heels. As the vikings rose, baying like hounds, the slaves dropped their burdens and their torches and ran screaming back to their boats. Some of them dived into the lake and began to swim for the other side, made afraid by the terrible appearance of the attackers.

Harald entered the cave five paces after Arkil, but even so was too late to save his friend. Grummoch was holding Arkil's body as though it had been a child's doll made from rags, swinging it like a bundle of straw, as he turned to face the onrush of vikings. And all saw, in the torchlight, that Arkil's brave head was loose on his neck. They had no further need to speculate on his fate.

As Harald ran whooping at the giant, Grummoch flung Arkil's body at him, sweeping the boy aside. But as Harald fell, he saw Haro Once-only, his sword between his teeth as he tore off his shirt, racing at the giant. There was a great roar, and then Harald got to his feet once more to see the vikings swarming round their gigantic opponent like hounds about a stag.

How long that grim battle went on, no one will ever know, but to all men who survived the affair, it seemed like a year rather than an hour.

Men flew hither and thither, once Grummoch could get a grip on them, and then lay gasping and coughing out their life on the floor of that terrible cavern. But at

last sheer weight of numbers bore the giant down, and Harald came suddenly behind him and struck him with all his force at the base of the neck with the flat of his sword.

Grummoch gave a loud groan and sank down, dragging six men with him. Goff Goffling, who fell beneath the giant in that tumble, gave a high shout and then lay still for ever.

In his berserker fury that Grummoch should have killed Arkil, Haro Once-only, whose right arm dangled limply by his side, would have run his sword through the giant with his left hand; but Harald stopped him, saying that they might use him as a beast of burden, if he was not wounded too badly.

The irony of this pleased the vikings, and they set to, to bind the giant with all the leg-strappings and ropes they could find.

And when the count of the dead was made, they found that they had bought their victory dearly, for of the sixteen northmen who had waited outside the cavern that night, only nine would live to share the treasure. Among the dead were Arkil, Goff Goffling, Sven Hawknose and Kran the Lark. Their comrades wept that such fine warriors should be sent packing to Valhalla so hurriedly, and without their treasure.

But when they carried the torches to the far end of the cavern and saw what they had gained by their battle, even those vikings who had loved the dead men best were forced to agree that such a price was not excessive for the riches that were now theirs.

Piled high against the far wall were sacks of Frankish

and English gold; goblets and trenchers of rich Byzantine ware; coronets and sceptres such as would have rejoiced the heart of a score of Caesars; and swords and scabbards of such richness that the vikings almost wept to see their flashing beauty.

Harald stood gazing, amazed, at the show before his eyes, when suddenly Grummoch began to groan and tried to sit up. Four of the vikings flung him back and sat on him to keep him down. He glared up at them and rolled his eyes horribly.

But at last he felt able to speak and then he said, 'It comes to every man that one day his dearest treasures shall be taken from him. I have worked hard for mine, but the will of the gods is stronger than my own arms. I do not complain. He who is strongest shall deserve the most. I am glad that I was beaten by real warriors, and not by the minions of that lap-dog MacMiorog; moreover, if the truth be told, I am glad that I put an end to so many before you others got me down. I can say no more.'

Then Harald replied, 'Grummoch, you speak like a true man and a great warrior. Will you come with us as a slave, or shall we put a sword into you now and have done with you? It is your right to choose.'

And then giant Grummoch said, 'It was foretold in my runes when I was a little lad that I should one day become a slave to men of three colours – golden, black, and red. You, I see, my boy, have golden hair, so that is the first part of my rune come to pass. I do not complain. Now let me rise.'

But the wily vikings would have none of that. Radbard Crookleg, who was skilled in blacksmithery, got out a

pair of gyves which he had forged the day before in Dun-
an-oir, and with the help of three others beat them on to
the ankles of Grummoch, who groaned loudly all the
while, saying that he would do them no harm if they let
him get up freely.

And when at last the job was done, they cut his bonds
and he rubbed his great arm muscles and grinned like
anyone else. He was in a way sorry, he said, to have killed
Arkil, for he had always had a soft spot for the Danish
Prince, although he had known all along that he must
one day kill him.

The vikings were sitting about in the cave, sharing
their dried meat with Grummoch, when suddenly the entrance was lit up with the flames from many torches.
King MacMiorog stood there, surrounded by his guards,
smiling evilly as he gazed at Grummoch.

Harald said, 'Well, King, we have captured your giant,
and now we shall go on our way with his treasure as we
arranged in your hall.'

But MacMiorog said, 'Yes, you will go on your way,
but without his treasure. For that I regard as being mine,
after all the suffering I have endured from this giant
these many years.'

Then he nodded to his guards and two of them stepped
forward, their swords drawn, to put an end to Grummoch.
But Harald and his men rose and stood before the giant,
to protect him.

'Step closer at your peril,' shouted Radbard, his smith's
hammer still in his hand. 'This giant is ours, to do with
as we please now, for he is our slave, and his treasure is
ours likewise.'

Then MacMiorog gave a shout of anger and called on his men to rush in and finish the vikings; but such was their fierce appearance in the torchlight, with the blood still on them, and their faces twisted in anger at the betrayal, that the King's men thought twice about it, and would not do as MacMiorog said.

So, followed by the taunts of the vikings, and the high-pitched laughter of the captive giant, the King and his men made their way back across the lake.

And when they had gone, Grummoch said, 'From now on he is your bitter enemy. He will poison you if you eat the food he offers. He will do all he can to kill you while you are in his land. Take my advice, and let us all go round to the back of the city without delay, for there are my own ox-wagons and oxen. We might well use them to get to wherever we are going, and for my own part, I should be glad of a change of scenery for this flat green plain is bad for my temper and my rheumatism.'

And so it was that the vikings loaded the treasure on to the rafts and at last on to the ox-wagons and set out towards the coast once more, even before the sun rose.

Their dead comrades they left in the cavern, lying side by side, each man holding his weapon so that he should be able to protect himself and his dead comrades in the long journey that must be made through the darkness to the land of everlasting light.

Grummoch agreed to roll the boulder back across the mouth of the cave, so that no man should ever disturb them again.

Chapter **6** *The Bargainers*

On the journey back to Murdea, it was agreed that Grummoch should be allowed to travel on one of the wagons, since his heavy leg-gyves made walking extremely painful to him. In return for this kindness, the giant went out of his way to make himself as friendly as possible to the vikings, sometimes playing to them on a little bone flute which he always carried, and on which he was a marvellously clever performer, and sometimes by telling them stories to while away the time. Usually, these tales were told in a high voice, punctuated by many interruptions when Grummoch stopped to laugh at one of his own jokes for he was an inveterate leg-puller, and for a giant had an amusing sense of humour.

Harald came to like him in the three days during which the wagon train wound its way towards the coast, and he would often sit alongside the giant, listening to his yarns.

He learned that Grummoch came from a poor farming family in Caledonia, one of many children, all the rest of them being of a normal size. When Grummoch was still small – only twice as big as he should have been – he had beaten many boys three times his age in fair fighting, but had always been thrashed when he got home for bullying his fellows. Also, he was in constant trouble for being greedy, when in fact he had eaten only half as much as he needed for that big body of his. He told Harald that from the start his mother hated him, for even as a baby he exhausted her, so that she could not carry him about or nurse him. Later, as he grew older, the other young lads of the steading refused to let him share their sports of wrestling or javelin-throwing because he always won; while the girls ran screaming from him if he asked them to dance in the harvest festivities.

The only thing his village would let him do was to work; and every farmer vied for his services when there was any manure to load, trees to cut down, grain to draw, ditches to dig. Yet though he did three times as much as a normal man, he was always cheated when it came to being paid, for it was commonly held in Grummoch's steading that the gods had given him a big body but a small brain.

Grummoch stood this treatment for some years, he told Harald, and then one day he decided he would not tolerate it any longer; so he began by filling the village pond with boulders which no men could ever drag out from the mud again; then he rolled two great hay-wains down a hill, breaking down twenty yards of dry stone walling in the process; after which he went into the church and pulled on the bell-ropes so hard that the top of the tower came down through the roof and shattered the font.

After that, he had to go on his travels, for all men's hands were turned against him. Even his mother shouted out down the road after him that she hoped never to see his evil face again.

'But,' said Grummoch almost tearfully as he told Harald of this, 'it comes on me more and more often that the one thing I would most love would be to see my dear mother again, before it is too late.'

Bit by bit, the vikings got the rest of his story; how he walked to the coast, stole a curragh and sailed it single-handed to Ireland; how he begged his bread there, playing on his flute and performing deeds of strength; how one day he overcame a great champion at a Fair in the Blue Mountains; and how at last he took service with King MacMiorog, and seeing that monarch's great luxury, decided that he too would amass such a fortune as would one day buy him a royal bride.

He ended his story by saying, 'And that was just what I had managed. It was her dowry that I was bringing home the night you attacked me. But for you, I might now be the son-in-law of the High King himself. Alas, alas!'

But Grummoch was by nature a light-hearted creature, and soon he was fluting again, as merrily as ever. Indeed, his company was so diverting that before the vikings reached Murdea again, their sorrow for the loss of Arkil and their comrades had much abated. For that was the way of life, they agreed; one met a man, and then lost him – all as Odin wished. It was best to accept what the gods decided, without complaining, for whether one wept or not, it made no difference. As for Grummoch, he had soon accepted the fact that his treasure was lost to him, but Harald told him that if he would come back with them to the village by the fjord, he would arrange it that old Thorn should accept him as a villager and should pay him a share equal to that which every other man would get; at which Grummoch seemed genuinely pleased.

Two miles out of Murdea, the wagon train came upon a party of Danes, who were riding on stolen horses inland. They were greatly interested in the giant and in the contents of the wagons, and when Harald told them the story, their greedy dark eyes lit up so brightly that had they not been put off by the looks of the wagon-party they would have attacked there and then.

Their leader, a gaunt-faced man called Riggall, said that he was anxious to profit even if only a little by the meeting, and suggested that since they would need a ship to carry their treasure home, he would sell them his ship, which lay in the harbour at Murdea, for one sack of treasure.

But Harald said, 'We too have a ship lying in the harbour at Murdea. It is a blackened hulk and lies at the bottom, among the eels. No doubt your ship lies alongside it, if we know anything of the people of that town!'

From the look on the Dane's face, the others could see that Harald's words had hit their target.

But the Dane was not to be beaten, 'Look you, bargainer,' he said, 'in three days, my own son-in-law, Borg, will pull into Murdea with a small ship, just such as could be managed by a small crew, as you yourselves are. Give him my ring, and tell him to sell you his boat fairly. Say that if he does not, I will give him a taste of my belt when I see him again.'

Harald took the ring and thanked him. The Dane held his hand for a moment and said, 'Is this not worth something, dear friend?' And he kept holding Harald's own hand so tightly that at last the boy signed to Grummoch, who flung the man a hunting-knife set with amber, and with a hilt carved in the shape of a prancing horse. This pleased the Dane so much that he shouted after them, 'And tell my son-in-law, Borg, that he must deal kindly with you or I will find my daughter another husband.'

So it was that they came to Murdea once more, to be met by a shower of arrows fired from the very church tower which they had spared on their way inland.

This time Radbard Crookleg was hurt in the neck. The shaft entered at one side and came out at the other. This angered his comrades so much that before Harald could stop them, they had barricaded the doors of the place, and, setting faggots of wood before it, had set light to it.

Grummoch consoled Harald on the way down to the harbour by saying that he had seen with his own eyes the priest and five men climb out of a little window at the back; so they at least would be safe.

'Why did you not tell the men, so that they could have driven them back into the flames?' asked Harald, wondering.

Grummoch shrugged his shoulders and took out his little flute. 'I am a Christian myself, Harald,' he said. 'Though I have always been rather a poor one, I fear.'

Then he began to play a restless little tune, and Harald could get no more out of him.

They camped at the harbour side, and suffered no more hurt from the men of Murdea, who were impressed by their fierce faces and fine weapons. On the third day, the Danish ship sailed in, and after Harald had given the Dane's message to Borg, the bargain was made, and the newcomers went on inland with half a sack of treasure and a full team of oxen and wagons.

Then, by common accord, Harald Sigurdson was named

the master of their new ship, which they joined in calling
Arkil the Prince, after their dead leader.

Harald said, 'By Odin, I swear to deal fairly with you
all, and as you deal fairly with me, so may we all prosper.
Has any man a word to say to that?'

As he waited for their answer, the gulls swirled over the
heads of the men in the bobbing longship, and the smoke
from the hovels at the waterside swept across the oily
swell.

All men were silent, save only Grummoch, who stretched and scratched himself noisily. 'Yes, shipmaster,' he
said, with a little smile 'I have a word to say.'

They looked at him in surprise.

'Say on, Grummoch, then,' said Harald.

And giant Grummoch yawned and said, 'My word is
this: let us set sail without any more talk! For I am
anxious to see this village of yours!'

Haro Once-only raised himself from his pallet of straw
on the deck and said grimly, 'That is well said, little giant;
for if you had spoken a word against Harald, Radbard and
I would have fed you to the seagulls.'

'Yes, in little pieces,' said Radbard in the high whistling voice that was his since his arrow-wound.

Then they all laughed and Grummoch said, 'Dear little
ones, you had better think about yourselves, for if you do
not get better soon, it is you who will go overboard to
feed the white chickens!'

Yet, in spite of the laughter and taunting, Radbard and
Haro were well cared for by the sea-rovers, for they were
brave comrades, and the first lesson a viking learned was
to stand by his ship-mates through thick and thin.

Haro's arm had been broken in the cavern-fight, but was now set in splints and gave him little discomfort provided that he did not roll on to it in the night. When that happened, the other vikings would clap their hands over their ears, in pretended horror at the things he would find to say.

As for Radbard, his wound had been less dangerous than had at first appeared, for the arrow had passed through the muscle of the neck and not through his gullet. All the same, the wound gave him so much pain while it was healing that he could only speak softly and on a high note, like a little girl – which went comically with his great hairy beard and his fierce face.

So it was, when they had stored their food and water under the after-deck of the ship, and had packed the treasure down snugly below the main-deck, wrapping it round with sacking and sheepskins, that they prepared to set forth. The great weight of the gold they carried caused them to ride low in the water, and they needed no further ballast.

'May Odin send us a safe crossing, without a storm,' said Olaf Redeye, cousin to Haro, 'for this is ballast which I would die rather than fling overboard !'

Giant Grummoch said pleasantly, 'You are very concerned about my treasure, little northman ! What about me, the founder of the hoard, how do you think I feel about losing it to you?'

Olaf said, 'We have an old saying : "A clean shirt to a pig; gold to a Pict." Neither of them understands the worth of such things, you see, Grummoch.'

Grummoch said, 'I cannot reach you, little Olaf, for

these gyves stop my free movement; but if you will come here to me, I will take you by the hand and show you what a friend I can be to you.'

He held out his massive hand, invitingly, but Olaf shook his head with a sly smile.

'Nay, Grummoch,' he said, 'but I need this hand for rowing, I thank you! Perhaps we will shake hands when we land in my country, for then my six brothers will be there to see that you let go when I yell!'

Grummoch nodded, reflectively, and said sadly, 'That is the trouble, no one will ever be my hand-friend. I once shook hands with a German bear, but he howled so loudly, I could not make myself heard when I asked him what was the matter.'

By this time Harald Sigurdson was at the steerboard, and called to them to take their places at the benches with the oars, for, he said, if they did not get started soon, they would have the good men of Murdea aboard to burn them off the face of the seas.

And certainly there was a nasty-looking crowd already assembled at the dockside, muttering and pointing angrily at the vikings. But Grummoch merely yawned again and called out to them, 'Would any of you brave souls like a little trip round the harbour before we start on our voyage? We will not charge you anything, and will set you safely ashore again when you have had enough!'

The men at the harbour's edge began to shout abuse at the vikings, so Grummoch called again, this time to the one who seemed to be their leader, 'You, good sir, with the bald head and the big nose, what about you? You look to be a rare sea-rover, will you not come with us?'

But he got no polite reply, and so, with stones and refuse whistling round their ears, the vikings set forth from Murdea, ten men in a little ship full of treasure, to make the long and tedious passage round the south coast of England, and up past the land of the Franks.

They put in for food once more at the Isle of Wight, and were not dissatisfied with the treatment they received there, for some of the islanders spoke a dialect similar to their own, having themselves come from Jutland many generations before.

So all went well for the first three days, but, early on the fourth, something happened which was to change the whole course of their lives.

It was a grey grim dawning, with bursts of rain scudding down from the north and the whipped ocean rolling strongly against the prow of the *Arkil*. The high sail was useless since the change of wind, and Harald and Grummoch pulled it down together, being buffeted mercilessly as they clung to the writhing canvas with frozen hands.

The other sea-rovers lay wrapped in their sheepskin cloaks, under the gunwales, sleeping as best they could, for their hands were already blistered with the rowing they had done the day before.

But Grummoch said, 'We shall have to waken them, shipmaster, for this is a wind that must be fought with more than snores!'

Harald woke Olaf only and asked him if he thought they might put ashore in the land of the Franks, at some quiet village, for example; but he shook his head and said grimly, 'Frank and northman, fire and water! I had as soon jump overboard now – they killed my father and three of my cousins last summer, trying to teach them to be Christians!'

So there was nothing for it but to wake the sleepers and set them rowing against the tide. Both Harald and Grummoch took turns at the oars, for with Radbard and Haro sick, they were short-handed.

But by midday, the weather grew worse, and soon a

great gale began to sweep out of the north, rendering the oarsmen as weak as kittens, drenching them through and filling their hearts with fear.

Haro called Harald over to him and said gloomily, 'It comes over me that we shall never get this treasure back to the fjord, shipmaster. It weighs the ship down, and soon we shall be foundering if these waves do not slacken. Besides, the boat is so heavy now that we need a crew of giants to move her through such a swell.'

Harald nodded, thoughtfully, and said, 'Let us have courage for a little while longer, Haro, and then, if we can do nothing better, we will lighten the load a little.'

He went back to his oar, but did not say anything about this conversation to the others, for they were all anxious, to a man, to get this great hoard back to their village and live lives of comfort evermore.

By early evening time, their next misfortune happened. Radbard went aft to broach a keg of water and came running back to say that it was all brackish and undrinkable. The men of the Isle of Wight had tricked them, it seemed, selling bad water for good gold, despite the similarity of the language they spoke.

Harald and Grummoch went aft to taste the water, and agreed that it would poison a man.

It was then that the gale caught them and drove them southwards like a leaf falling from a high oak-tree, powerless, swirling hither and thither, out of control. Harald shrieked for the men to draw in their oars, but his words came too late; three oars were swept away, out of the weakened hands of the rowers.

So, as night came on, the *Arkil* went her own way, far

off the course Harald had set, until at last Radbard cried out that if the storm did not die away soon, they would eat their next meal in Africa.

He was not far wrong. The storm grew from fury to fury, throughout the night, and all through the next day, lashing the little longship as though it was a hated thing, almost turning it turtle a hundred times, snapping off the mast, breaking in the gunwales on one side, and straining the stout oak strakes to the utmost of their strength.

Now the battered vikings had no heart left for anything but to huddle close to each other, in whatever shelter they could find, which was little enough. Even the stoutest stomached of them had been sick, and not a man but was frozen until he could hardly speak.

Then, as the utterly chill dawn of the third day struck across their ravaged deck, the wind fell and the seas rolled back to their accustomed places. And far on the steerboard bow, Harald at last sighted a thin grey shape low on the horizon.

'Yes, that is land,' said Grummoch, 'though who should know which land it is, we have been so buffeted ! And I for one do not care which land it is, for if we can only reach it, I will never set foot on a ship's deck again.'

And others, even the hardiest of the vikings, said the same thing.

Then the problem was taken out of their hands, for on the larboard beam and bow suddenly appeared three ships, long and low in the water, gliding towards them like sea snakes, catching the morning wind in their triangular red sails.

Harald rubbed his eyes and said, 'I have never seen

such ships before; they are built for speed and even if we
had our sail and our oars, we could not escape them.'

Radbard, who stood with him at the gunwales said in
his high voice, 'It is not the ships which worry me, it is
their crews. Look, they are little dark men, not sea-rovers
at all.'

Grummoch shaded his eyes and there was fear in his
voice as he spoke. 'We can expect no mercy from them,
my friends,' he said. 'I know their like. For the love of
god, strike off these gyves so that I can at least defend
myself when they draw alongside.'

Then, to the horror of all the vikings, Harald said, 'We
have no hammer, Grummoch. It went overboard in the
night and I could not save it.'

At this, Grummoch gave a great cry and jumped overboard. Radbard tried to stop him, putting out his hand,
but it would have been as easy to hold back an oak, falling
in a high wind.

'He will drown, with those leg-gyves on,' groaned Radbard. 'His ghost will never let me rest for what I did to
him.'

But Haro said, 'You should be worrying about your
own ghost, my friend, not Grummoch's, for the men who
are coming to board us do not carry bunches of flowers in
their hands!'

Now Grummoch had disappeared among the breakers,
and the vikings turned, to sell their lives as dearly as their
failing strength would let them, each armed with a
weapon from the store they had taken from the cave.

And as the sharp-prowed ships cut in at them from all
directions, their gunwales lined with dark-faced men,

Radbard shouted suddenly, 'They may take our heads, but they shall not take our gold!'

Then, before anyone could stop him, he had torn back the plank that led beneath the deck, and all men saw him give a great heave at the oak bung in the ship's bottom.

The green sea rushed in, ice-cold and hungry, about the waists of the vikings in a flash.

'Radbard, you fool!' shouted Harald, as he saw the man flung down beneath the deck planks by the onrush of water.

Then they were in the sea, with the *Arkil* sucking at them as she sank, and the three cruel-looking ships above them, treading them down into the waters it seemed, and the little dark men grinning above them, their white teeth gleaming in the early morning sunlight.

Chapter **8** *Slave Market*

For years afterwards, the events which followed came to
Harald like a strange dream; first someone leaning down
and trying to pull him up into the boat, then the sensa-
tion of falling again, clutching out and missing his hold,
and then the green swirl of waters above him while the
harsh keel of the boat rolled over him, forcing him down
and down, until he thought that his lungs would burst.
Then, at last, coming back from a dark and rushing
nightmare to find himself lying on a white-scrubbed deck
in the sunshine, between two rows of black-legged rowers
and the taut red sail above him, bellying in a following
wind ... And, best of all, Radbard and Haro lying beside
him.

It was some time before Harald discovered that his legs
were bound – and that none of the rest of his crew besides
Radbard and Haro had been picked up. When he knew
that, his sunlit mood turned to one of black despair.

Radbard, who had miraculously shot up to the surface
when the *Arkil* sank, was grim and tongue-tied; Haro sat
nursing his aching arm, too deep in despair to speak, even
to his dear friends.

Shortly after Harald's senses had returned to him, a tall
man dressed in a long white robe and wearing a red turban came down between the sweating oarsmen and
kneeled beside him. Harald noted that his long brown

fingers were covered with gold rings and that his curved sword had an exquisite hilt of chiselled steel, set with amethysts.

The man smiled at him, showing his perfectly white teeth, and began to speak to him in a soft and musical voice. But his words were strange and Harald could not understand him. The man made several attempts to make his meaning clear, but Harald shook his head.

At last the man shrugged his shoulders and began to make signs. He pointed to the hide bonds which fastened Harald's ankles, then he made the motion of counting out money from one hand to the other. Harald understood. 'You want us to pay you to let us free?' he asked.

But the other did not understand and smiled, nodding his head.

Then, with a cold shudder, Harald said, 'Are we slaves?'

The man heard the one word, and nodded happily, 'Slaves,' he said, recognizing that single word, 'Slaves, you slaves!'

Radbard heard this and turned away with a groan. Haro put up his good hand to his eyes for they had filled with tears.

Harald clenched his teeth and said to the man, 'If I had a sword I would give you the payment you deserve.'

But the man still smiled and shook his head, not understanding. Then, seeing that he would get no further with these three rough bears of the north, he shrugged his shoulders as though he had done all he could and went back to the helm, swinging the long narrow ship towards the shore, which rapidly grew nearer and nearer, until

Harald could actually distinguish the shapes of gaily clothed men and women moving in the sunshine before the white houses.

Soon after that they were running in alongside a low jetty, and then that same man with the red turban came to them and indicated with his long white staff that they were to disembark. But this time he did not smile, and when Radbard rose slowly, he felt the weight of that white stick, suddenly and viciously. Harald stopped, aghast, and then, with a slow cold anger, turned and struck the man a blow with his clenched fist between the eyes.

'No man shall treat my crew like that while I am here to prevent it,' said Harald, glaring round him. But Radbard shook his head gravely. 'That was a daring thing to do, Harald,' he said. 'Now look what the results may be.'

The tall man sprawled on the sun-dried planking of the jetty, holding his head and speaking to his followers in a vicious tone of voice. These followers ran immediately to do his bidding, and soon came back from a shed with a smouldering brazier.

Haro said listlessly, 'It would seem to be their custom to brand rebellious slaves. I had not thought to be branded when I set out from Murdea with my share of the treasure glittering in my dreams. Alas, but a man's life is quite unpredictable!'

Radbard said, 'I have a dragon tattooed in the middle of my chest. I hope these fellows do not mar the design with their clumsy botching. What do you say if we offer to brand each other, to see that the job is done properly?'

Then they were dragged forward, towards the brazier.

A thick-armed man bent over it, blowing the coals to white heat with a little sheepskin bellows. They saw that an iron lay in the fire, getting hotter and hotter. A small crowd of men and women had gathered now, anxious not to miss any entertainment that might be offered by the slaves, and the man in the red turban, who had now regained his former air of authority after his blow on the head, was talking excitedly to the crowd, explaining some point or other, which necessitated his waving his hands violently up and down.

Harald said, 'I think he is telling them that we deserve the punishment. He wishes them to think him a just man, doubtless.'

Radbard said, 'It comes to me, from the look of these folk and the shape of their houses, that we must be in that part of Spain where the Moors have come to live. And if that is so, then we must expect to find them a very just people, for their Caliphs make strict laws, causing them to be respected in this part of the world. We can look for justice, no doubt.'

Haro grinned and pushed away a man who had gripped him too strongly by the shoulder of his injured arm. 'Yes, but what if we do not care for their justice, friend?'

Harald said, 'We are northmen, not Moors, Radbard. Our justice is what I would go by, not theirs. Besides, he deserved the blow I gave him, according to any man's justice, for he struck you when you were unable to move any faster.'

Radbard smiled and said, 'Very well, you are the shipmaster and I obey your orders. What shall we do?'

Harald said, 'We must make it unpleasant for them if

they try to harm us. That is as far as I can think, with these three ruffians hanging on to my arms.'

Suddenly a great hush fell on the chattering crowd, and then the man in the red turban gave a signal to the guards who held Harald. They dragged him towards the brazier and then waited. The man in the red turban spoke harshly to the one who bent over the flames, and as he straightened, the hot iron in his hand, Harald gave a great cry, 'Up the North!'

He heard his cry echoed by Haro and Radbard, behind him, and then he lunged forward with all his strength, snapping the hide thong which held his ankles. He felt the thing go, and with his new freedom he kicked out, catching the brazier with the side of his foot and scattering the coals among the crowd. He heard men and women cry in sudden alarm, and then he had shaken himself free, and was punching out to left and right. He had time to see that Haro and Radbard were doing the same, and then, overpowered by sheer weight of numbers, Harald sank down to the ground, half-suffocated by the Moorish sailors who clutched him wherever they could get a hold.

For a moment, he saw nothing but legs and feet, and was momentarily afraid that they might trample him to death. Then he heard a strong voice cutting through all the hubbub, and suddenly he found himself free again, and looking up at a short, squat man who wore a round helmet and an iron breastplate, and whose skin was very much lighter than that of the pirates who had captured him. This man's high boots were of the old Roman pattern, as was his short purple cloak and the broad sword which swung in a moroccan leather scabbard at his right side. He seemed to be a man of power, from the way in which he addressed the pirate captain in the red turban.

Harald could not understand his speech, for he spoke the Arabic of the Moors; yet even Harald could recognize that his manner of saying the words was not that of the sea-rovers who had bound him and brought him to this place.

Suddenly, when all was still again, the man touched Harald in the side with the toe of his fine riding-boot and said, 'Well, and is this the sort of behaviour one would expect from a slave?'

Harald stared at him in wonder for he spoke the tongue of the north – though not like a northman, but like one who had learned the words in his travels there.

Harald stared him in the eye and said, 'I am Harald Sigurdson, a shipmaster. These men have attacked my ship, *Arkil*, and have caused us to scuttle her off this coast. Now they treat us like beasts.'

The man nodded and said, 'You are their rightful prize, my good fellow; they are slave-runners and do not go out to sea for the fun of it. They plan to sell you in the slave market, at a good price, for you are all young men and have plenty of work left in you, if a man only knows how to fetch it out of you !'

The man in the red turban now came forward and began to argue with the other, who answered him in Arabic. At length the newcomer turned and said to Harald, 'This captain says he wishes to punish you all for your rebellious behaviour, to leave such a mark on you as will warn other good men that you are savage beasts and must be watched.'

Harald answered, 'Then he is a fool, for we only did what any warrior would do, no more. We are not savage beasts, but good northmen, whose only wish is to go about our own business without interference from any man.'

The man in the helmet tugged at his dark beard and smiled a little grimly. 'I am a Frank,' he said, 'and so I have some knowledge of you good northmen, and of the business you like to go about!'

Radbard broke in, saying, 'What, you a Frank, and you side with these heathen?'

The man said, 'I was captured in battle, my friend, and so became a slave, as you are. But my master, Abu Mazur, is an enlightened man; he used me sensibly, making me his emissary up and down the land, for this and that. I am contented. I have known worse masters, and Christian ones at that.' He paused for a moment and then smiled and said, 'You should have no cares about my fate, for after all you too are heathen, my friends!'

Harald said, 'Look you, master Frank, we are in a sad plight. Let us have done with talk of heathen and such like. Will you help us?'

The other smiled and nodded. 'I shall, my friend,' he said. 'For I shall buy the three of you now, if I can get you at a reasonable price, and if you will promise me that you will not get up to your berserk tricks as soon as you leave this place.'

Harald answered, 'I do not like being a slave, but you seem a fair-minded man for a Frank, and I will promise that we will not try to break your neck, or even to run away for the time being. Is that enough?'

The man nodded and added, 'If you break your word, it will go uncomfortably with you, one way and another. I say no more; Abu Mazur is a good master but a cruel enemy. That is his rule of life.'

Then he left the vikings and began to bargain with the man in the red turban.

And so it was that soon they were dragged to their feet and had their wrists tied tightly with thin hide thongs. Then they were pushed towards the man in the helmet, who mounted his black mule and turning said, 'Follow me without causing any disturbance. My wagon train waits at the outskirts of this town. We have a long journey to make.'

They did as they were told. On reaching the busier part of the town, they came upon a broad square, set round with many-coloured awnings.

'Is this a market?' asked Radbard, who thought they might buy food.

'Yes,' answered the Frank, smiling down on them from his saddle. 'Look at the merchandise they sell here and be thankful.'

The wondering vikings did as they were told and stared at the bright stalls. Under every awning sat a slave-master, with his wares: men and women and children of all races, it seemed, and all tongues. There were bright-haired children from England, standing sullenly and glowering at these foreigners who inspected them as though they had been pigs at a Fair; red-haired Caledonians, who pulled away and bared their teeth whenever a prospective buyer went towards them; great laughing Africans, who went out of their way to attract a kind-faced purchaser; small

slant-eyed Tartars, who squatted nonchalantly, as though they were at home, and did not seem to care what happened to them as long as they were alive; restless lithe Armenians, who held out their delicate hands to passers-by, asking to be bought and fed.

Radbard said that he thought he saw three northmen, who had once sailed with him beyond Orkney, but the Frank said that he did not mean to buy any more northmen that day. Three were enough, he said, and if they protested, he would sell them back into this market and have done with it.

They did not protest, but walked on with him to the outskirts of the town. And there, drawn up beside a wayside inn, were the four wagons, with their patient oxen already in the harness, waiting to go. Harald noted grimly that a dozen riders, with lances, accompanied the wagon-train, so that all thoughts of an escape while on the journey faded from his mind.

Then they were told to get into the first wagon, which they did without further protest. In it were three Bulgar boys, who wept incessantly. The vikings tried to console them, but found that it was impossible to do so; the Bulgars seemed to enjoy their grief more than their consolation. So, since the wagon was thickly laid with straw, and since they were still fatigued from their long sea journey, the vikings gave up trying to help their fellow-slaves, and curled up, like dogs, and fell asleep.

When they awakened, it was almost evening time and the red sun struck sadly over the harsh countryside, showing them the nature of the land they had come to – a great, undulating plain, with sharply serrated hills on the skyline; a place of small, dried-up bushes and great fissures in the reddish earth. A place where the sun shone down unmercifully in the day, and the frosts broke up the soil cruelly in the night.

The Frank brought them a dish of broken meat and a pannikin of harsh red wine each. Then they went back to sleep, lulled by the rocking of the wagon.

It was to be a long journey, down to the truly Muslim south, where the Moors had settled in their many thousands, bringing their language and their customs from the east, setting up their bulwark of Islam in the western world.

And it was to this strange world that the three exhausted viking sea-rovers were now travelling, slowly, inevitably and sadly; three free men who were now slaves; three men who had recently been as rich as Caesars and were now poorer than the poorest goosegirl along the far northern fjords.

Harald once said this to Haro, on the journey; but Haro only turned over in the straw to find a more comfortable spot and muttered thickly, 'The black beetle climbs up the table-leg, but there is a hand waiting to crush him when he reaches the top.'

Part Two

Chapter **9** *The House at Jebel Tarik*

Autumn passed, and then slow-footed winter. Now, with the coming of spring and the reopening of trade in the Mediterranean, the great white house of Abu Mazur was a hive of activity, for the Master himself was coming down from his winter residence to be near his galleys and his ledgers, at Jebel Tarik.

The three vikings stood on the high terrace that looked down on to the busy harbour. They saw the red flowers in their gilded urns, hanging heavily over the marble balustrade, teased by the light spring breezes; they saw the many broad white steps that led down and down and down, until they were as small as steps in a dream, to the broad and crowded wharf, where Abu Mazur's heavily-laden galleys bobbed lazily on the blue tide, waiting the signal that would send them to far Cyprus, or Crete, or even to Byzantium.

Harald stood gazing at the ships, tugging impatiently at his long golden plaits; in his mind's eye he saw himself, with his companions, in the prow of such a ship, cleaving through the blue waters to freedom, to adventure, to far Miklagard itself . . .

Haro came up to him and touched his arm. 'Do not brood, shipmaster,' he said gently. 'The captive wolf wears out his heart walking round his cage; you are a man, not a wolf; do not wear out your heart, Harald.'

Harald turned away from his friend with a great sigh. Haro shrugged his shoulders and began to flick pebbles over the edge of the balustrade, on to the broad white steps. They bounded down and down, until they were impossible to see for their smallness in the distance. Sometimes the cluster of guards who always stood half-way up the steps glared back as the stones passed by them, looking up at the vikings with annoyance showing on their dark fierce faces. Once a pebble struck one of these men, a great fellow wearing a gilded helmet with a tall yellow plume. He swung round and shouted at Haro, shaking his long curved sword at him. But Haro only smiled sadly and then flicked another pebble. He knew that the soldiers were not permitted to come through the upper gateway and on to the terrace. He knew also that house slaves were considered as men of some importance and must not be beaten by mere soldiers. The Frankish Captain, Clothair, had told him as much.

Clothair had been very helpful, in his rough way; he had seen that the three vikings were given easy tasks, indoors, and had even sent a teacher to them, to give them at least a little insight into the Arabic tongue. This had helped to keep their minds occupied during the long winter days and nights.

Now at last they were to see Abu Mazur, the Great One, the richest merchant of Jebel Tarik, their master.

Radbard said, 'I have been dreaming of my house by the fjord these last few nights, Harald. My mother will be missing me now that the sowing-time has come again. Since my father died, I alone have put the barley seeds in the ground, and my mother will expect me to do it this year too. She will not let my cousins do it; she says the seed would never grow if such young ruffians laid their hands on it.'

Harald said sadly, 'You will not be there to do it this year, Radbard.'

Radbard thought for a moment and then said, 'I have been thinking, Harald, that if we could get past the guards, we might hide in one of those great ships and at last sail away from here.'

Haro shook his head and said grimly, 'Radbard, my friend, no men, not even men like us, could pass those guards down there; and even if they could, there are more guards at the bottom step, and yet more guards on the wharf. There must always be at least a score of guards between us and the wharf; a man would need the hammer of Thor to make his way to the ships.'

Radbard said, 'Perhaps, perhaps, Haro; then might we not go out the other way, through the house?'

Harald smiled ruefully and said, 'That is worse; we do not know our way. There are many courtyards, and passages, and high walls. One room leads into another and then another, and that into a courtyard, and that into more rooms, until a man might go mad, trying to find his way outside. I was lost there once, myself, when the slave-master sent me with a message to one of the cooks. Luckily, Clothair found me, and brought me back to my sleeping-place, or I would have beaten my head on the wall with hopelessness.'

Haro nodded his agreement. 'Yes,' he said, 'I have seen the places you speak of, and there are guards everywhere, in niches, in towers, on the walls, in the courtyards; everywhere. It is not possible.'

Radbard turned away from them without saying any more.

Haro came up to Harald and whispered, 'I do not like the way friend Radbard is looking, shipmaster. He means to run away, of that I am sure. And if he does that, then he is as good as a dead man.'

Harald nodded. 'Yes,' he replied. 'That thought was in my own mind about him. But what can we do?'

Haro answered with a grim little smile, 'Once, I would not have thought twice about the problem; I should have gone with him, against all the odds in Islam, against all the Moors in creation. But now, with an arm that will not always do what I bid it do, and a heart that has been softened by the good food and drink of this place, I hesitate. Yes, I too wish to see the north again, but not from above, as a spirit in the air ! When I go to the fjord once more, I wish to greet my friends as a man, like them !'

They would have gone on discussing this for a long while, for the northmen loved argument, but just then the silver trumpet blew within the house, and then there was a great shouting and a scurrying of feet. The slave-masters were runing out on to the platform where the three friends were, urging the many slaves of the house to hurry and assemble there in neat rows, for the Master, Abu Mazur himself, was already at the main gate, and coming to inspect his new stock as the first thing he did on his arrival from his winter residence.

The vikings kept together, standing with the others in the second row – Romans, Turks, Franks, Africans – all whispering in their excitement, in their many tongues, for this was a great occasion.

Harald saw that Clothair was waiting by the inner door, his helmet carrying a new red plume, his breastplate burnished until it sent off blinding rays in the morning sunlight. Then the trumpet blew again, but more softly this time, and Clothair suddenly fell to his knees beside the door, bowing his head until the red plume almost touched the white marble flagstones of the terrace. Abu Mazur appeared.

He was an old man, but still very upright and dignified in his bearing. His high turban, surmounted by a silver cross set within a crescent moon, made him look even taller than he was; as did his long, sky-blue robe, which reached down in straight folds to his feet. His thin, bejewelled hand rested on the silver pommel of his curved scimitar. His long, noble face, its narrow chin fringed with a wisp of grey beard, was set in gently quizzical lines, which were etched deeply in the sallow skin, giving him a curiously humorous look. He was most obviously a man of great wealth and power, yet a man of simple but refined tastes, and a man of good humour.

He paused for an instant and spoke to Clothair, bidding him get up from his knees and explain which were the new slaves who must be inspected.

Clothair rose but did not move when his master moved. Then the vikings saw that he was waiting for someone else to pass through the pointed doorway before he followed Abu Mazur. It was a young girl of not more than sixteen years, who walked with the lazy grace of a panther, secure in the knowledge of her father's wealth and power. A tall Nubian who stood next to Harald whispered, 'That is Marriba, the Master's only child. She will be a princess one day, perhaps a Queen, who knows? He would lay down his life for her, my fellows.'

Haro sucked in his breath and said dreamily, 'I think that I would lay down mine for that lady. She is the most beautiful one it has been my fortune to set eyes on.'

Harald smiled at him and whispered, 'Wait till I tell the girls of our village by the fjord, Haro the Heartless! They will pull your plaits off in their jealousy!'

But Haro went on gazing at Marriba, sighing all the time, as though he were not a warrior but a silly little boy outside a sweetmeat booth on a Fair day.

Yet Harald had to agree that Marriba was a most impressive creature; though she was young, yet her almond-shaped face had an air of dignity beyond her years. Her skin was of a light golden colour, her hair as black as the raven's wing, her eyes great and round, fringed with dark lashes, soft as the doe's eyes, yet capable of flashing with anger it seemed.

Harald said softly to Radbard, 'It comes into my mind that I would like to see a girl of the north now, my friend; someone with long flaxen hair and sky-blue eyes; someone whose skin was like cream, not dark ivory.'

Radbard shrugged and said, 'I am only interested in the seas and the forests and the fjords; I do not worry my head over skin like dark ivory, my friend.'

Then the two great ones were almost beside them, and Clothair gave Harald a warning glance, to show him that he must keep silent until Abu Mazur had passed.

But Abu Mazur did not pass so easily. Instead, when he

stood opposite Harald, he stopped and looked the young viking up and down.

'Are these the seacocks from the north?' he asked the Frank.

Clothair bowed and nodded. Abu Mazur stood still, fingering his grey beard with long fingers, his surprisingly dark eyes fixed on Harald's. Harald stared back at him, wondering why this old man should concern himself to look so long into a slave's face.

Then Abu Mazur said, 'You are a bold young man, I can see that. Who is your father? He must be a great warrior.'

Harald stood up as straight as he could and looked above the Moor's head.

'My father was Sigurd of the three swords. He was the greatest warrior of his lord's host. He was the bravest seafarer along the fjords. Now he is gone and his only son is a slave among folk who hold to other gods.'

Abu Mazur considered him for a whole minute, never taking his dark eyes from the young man's face. Then, his voice very quiet, he said, 'And does his only son consider that he is a warrior, too?'

Harald thought that there was the slightest taunt in the words and he replied with heat, 'Give me a sword and I will meet any two of your guard here, on the steps, in return for the freedom of my two companions.'

Abu Mazur smiled and nodded his head. 'I had heard that you northfolk were great bargainers, and it seems to be true. Well, I will take your word for it that you are what you say, for I cannot allow my slaves to fight with my guards, who are all valuable and highly-trained soldiers and needed for other things. But I will do one thing for you; I will allow you to do that work in my house which best suits you. Now what task would you prefer, son of Sigurd?'

Harald's mouth became a thin hard line. He said abruptly, 'I am no slave to work in other men's houses. I am a warrior and a sea-captain. I know nothing of maids' work.'

Abu Mazur's grave face still kept its deep lines of humour, but his dark eyes seemed to shroud at these words, and something harder seemed to come into them. He passed by Harald without saying another word. But he stopped once again before Radbard and said gently, 'What is in your mind, northman?'

Radbard said simply, 'In my mind there is nothing but the sea and the planting of the barley seed, master.'

Abu Mazur answered just as simply, 'I cannot give you the sea, but you shall plant what seed we have.'

Then he passed on along the line and they lost sight of him as he turned to the other slaves.

But Marriba stayed behind a moment longer, looking Harald straight in the eye with her own great eyes. She smiled, ever so little, and said softly, 'You crow loudly, seacock; I wonder if you can peck as well?'

This made the other slaves laugh, and Harald was angry for an instant. Then he shrugged and looked away from her, afraid that he might say something which he would regret later.

Later that morning, as the three vikings sat on the steps, trying to scratch runes on the marble with sharp pebbles, a little hunched man came to them, his head shrouded in a massive turban, his body clothed in a much-patched shirt. He spoke harshly, as one who addresses his inferiors. 'Come with me,' he said, 'the Master has given me command over you. I am the gardener and you are to serve me in the garden of the great courtyard.'

The vikings halted in their scribbling and then, ignoring him, went on with their scratching. The little man jumped with rage.

'Come, when I command,' he said, 'or I will see to it that you are well punished. You will get to know soon enough that I am a person of some power in this house.'

Haro was nearest to him, sprawling on the white steps and trying to draw a ship with the wind full in the sail. It was the only thing he could draw, and he always took great pains over getting every strake drawn correctly, though without much imagination. So the gardener's words passed over Haro's head; he did not even bother to look up.

But suddenly the little man's foot came down on Haro's hand as he drew, harshly and cruelly.

'Let me show you what manner of man I am,' shouted the gardener.

Haro stared at his bruised knuckles for a moment, then, rising slowly, reached out and took the man by the neck and the leg. He held him for a moment, then calmly leaned over the balustrade with him. The guards below looked very small and far away. Their words did not reach the top of the stairs though they talked loudly.

The gardener began to cry hoarsely.

Haro said, 'And now let this show you what manner of man I am!'

He made to swing the gardener out into space, above the dark blue sea. Harald and Radbard sat looking at this, smiling all the time, the pebbles still in their hands.

Then suddenly Haro swung the little man back on to the steps and let him fall roughly on the marble. He lay

there for a while, his hand clasped to his heart, as though he expected it to fail at any moment, his brown eyes wide with terror still at the memory of that long sheer drop.

Then Haro knelt gently beside him and said, 'If a northman had trodden on my sword hand as you did a moment ago, he would now lie dead, with such wounds on his body as would frighten a dragon to dream of ! Are you not lucky, O little gardener-man?'

The man tried to speak, but could not get his breath.

Haro went on, 'Know then, little gardener-man, that from now on you are graced by the company of great warriors, who will deal harshly with you if you so much as raise your voice to them again !'

He waited for a moment, until the man had regained his breath.

'Now, good little gardener-man, lead on and we will follow; but see that you set us gentle work to do, or by Odin, I will drag you from your bed one night and finish the journey I was about to send you on today. Come on, get up and we will follow you !'

The man needed no second bidding, but did as Haro had said. So the vikings became gardeners in the house at Jebel Tarik, all because Radbard had had a desire to plant the barley along the fjord, as he had always done since his father, Radbard the Horse's Face, had passed away to Valhalla.

The great courtyard was a most magnificent place. It stood in the utmost centre of the vast house of Abu Mazur and was the joy of his heart, next to his beautiful daughter, Marriba.

Its broad floor was paved with porcelain tiles of many colours, laid out in the coiling arabesques of a Persian rug. In the centre of the tiled space was a fountain, made of alabaster and edged with beaten silver, in the shape of a snake coiling round a pomegranate, the sparkling water issuing from the snake's upturned mouth.

On all four sides of the tiled space were arcades, formed by arches of terra cotta, supported by veined marble pillars of such slenderness that one stood amazed that these delicate stalks should carry such weight.

Within each arch was a garden box of black marble, its sides overflowing with the luxuriantly flowering plants – red, yellow, blue, purple, orange and violet, so that the cool air was always filled with the scent of blossom.

This courtyard was not open to the sky, but had a double canopy, the upper sheet of which was of thick samite, striped with red and gold; and the lower sheet of which was of a delicate thin-spun silk, almost transparently woven. This allowed the light to come down from above, while keeping off the strongest blows of the sun at midday. It also had this purpose, that it allowed one to observe the colours and the flights of the many

captive birds which were kept there, within the two sheets
– whose voices, mingling with the voice of the fountain
and of the small aeolian harps set on the roof, gave to this
courtyard an air of Paradise.

When Radbard first entered the place, he shrank back
almost in fear and gasped, 'No, not yet! I have not died
yet – or have I?'

After Harald had assured him that he was still flesh and
blood, Radbard said, 'But it is impossible. When I said I
wanted to plant seeds, I meant on a wind-swept upland,
with the salt in my face, strong hairy barley seed that
doesn't mind if a bullock tramples on it; not this sort of
garden, where the flowers are like delicate princesses who
would shrink from the touch of such rough hands as mine!'

Haro said, 'We shall get used to it, friend! It is like
fighting in a battle; the first time one sweats and can
hardly hold one's sword still. But after that, one talks to
one's side-fellow as one advances, discussing the weather,
the crops, the next feast, and so on.'

Harald said, 'You both talk like old women; I am all
for doing something useful. Come, the water is cool and
our feet are hot; let us wash them, that makes good sense.'

So the three vikings took off their heavy goatskin shoes
and bathed their tired feet in the rich fountain, while the
little hunched man who was their master wrung his
hands in fear lest Abu Mazur should pass through the
courtyard while they were about their ablutions. But the
vikings ignored him, and Abu Mazur did not pass
through the courtyard so all went well.

Nevertheless, Marriba, who was watching them
through the grille of an upper window saw it all, and told

her father, who smiled and said, 'They are three devils, my daughter, and I do not know what I shall do with them. Perhaps I shall come to like them one day – and perhaps I shall have to turn them over to the executioner. Who knows?'

Marriba pouted and said, 'But father, do not let us dispose of them until they have entertained us a little more. They are droll, these bears of the north! We have never had such funny ones before.'

Her father had given her a wry look and then turned back to his accounts, which were long and tedious, since he was so wealthy and involved in business. He was not the sort of man who leaves all his affairs to a secretary; for, as Abu Mazur knew well enough, in such matters no secretary is ever as trustworthy as one is oneself.

So life went on quite smoothly for the three sea-rovers, at their work or their rough play in the great courtyard. Their work was very light and consisted mainly in watering the many plants and in sweeping and keeping clean the bright tiles of the place. Sometimes this became tiresome to the vikings and then the master gardener was teased without mercy and more than once was held, head downwards, over the fountain, when he had spoken too irritably to one or other of his slaves.

Once Haro said, 'I pity that little gardener-man. If I were such a man, I think I would swallow that prickly cactus and so put an end to my worries!'

'I cannot understand why he does not report us to Clothair and get us whipped or put on to a heavier task,' said Harald. 'There is something strange in our being allowed to stay here after the things we do.'

Radbard said, 'There is nothing strange in it. If he were to tell Clothair, then he would be punished or his position taken from him, for not keeping better order. That is all.'

Nevertheless, the antics of the vikings had been observed by one pair of sharp eyes, and Abu Mazur's mind had been troubled to think that there was any sort of disobedience among his slaves. The result was that one day the three vikings came to work in their courtyard to find three well-armed guards lolling against the pillars, seemingly resting from more arduous duties outside.

Haro went up to their leader and said insolently, 'Good day, General. You appear to be fatigued, my friend. Would you care for a dip in the fountain? It is most refreshing, I do assure you.'

The guard, who was a massive man, stared down at Haro from beneath his heavily-lidded eyes, then, showing his white teeth as he spoke, said, 'I am not Rajik, the little gardener, my friend. I am a warrior and I do not make a habit of letting rug-headed barbarians up-end me over fountains. Go back to your tasks, or you may feel the butt-end of my lance in a place where you would not find it welcome!'

Haro stepped back a pace and said gently, with a slow smile on his face, 'Now I am nearer to you, I notice that you smell, dear Captain. Let me repeat that a wash would do you no harm.'

Harald ran forward now and tried to drag Haro away, but he set his feet resolutely and would not budge, not even for his friend.

The guard still lolled against his pillar, but with a

slight movement of his hip swung his heavy dagger round to a position where he could reach it easily.

'Go back to your tasks, slave, and do not meddle with affairs which might bring your stay here to an abrupt conclusion,' he said. Now Harald was greatly worried for he saw that Haro's face had begun to twitch and that he was tugging at the short plaits which hung beside his ears, things which always happened when the man was about to run berserk.

He stepped forward to grasp Haro, but even as he did so, the viking launched himself at the great soldier, taking him off his balance and tumbling him on to the gay tiles of the courtyard.

Haro was about to leap on to him, but Harald saw that, if he did, he would be jumping to his death for the soldier had drawn his dagger and was holding it upwards so that the viking would fall upon it.

Then behind them there was a scuffling of feet and Harald turned to see the other guards running across the courtyard.

At the same time, Radbard thrust a sweeping broom into Harald's hand, and offered another to Haro, who stood breathing fiercely, willing to grasp any weapon which might aid him against the guard.

And at that point, Marriba, opening her window to find out what the noise meant, saw the three great vikings, standing in a triangle, and warding off the blows rained on them by the guards, whose weapons were long narrow-bladed axes, set with sharp spikes.

'Quickly, quickly, father,' she called. 'Here is a sight one does not see every day!'

She jumped with excitement, like a little girl, when

Harald suddenly bent his head to let an axe sweep over him, and then, with a lightning movement, brought up the end of his broom into his opponent's body. The man staggered back and fell into the fountain, winded.

At this Haro gave a great laugh and brought down his broom-handle fair and square on the right shoulder of his guard, causing the man to drop his weapon, and fall back, groaning with pain.

Radbard had seen these things and, anxious not to be outdone by his companions, was driving his opponent before him, as a dog might drive a rabbit.

Haro and Harald were laughing and shouting now, forgetful of their situation, when suddenly the voice of Abu Mazur came down to them, commanding and hard.

'Stop, this instant, all of you,' he said. 'The next man to strike a blow will row out the rest of his life in my prison galley!'

The men all looked up at the window where their master stood, his lean face working with anger. The guards picked up their weapons and stood sheepishly beside the vikings, their heads bowed in shame.

Harald stared back at Abu Mazur, defiantly, but now even Harald felt the great strength of the other's eyes and looked down, to see Marriba smile suddenly, a small and impertinent smile, as though she was saying that her father held no terrors for her, and that she would see that all went well.

Later, standing before Abu Mazur in his small room, the vikings heard him say, 'My house is a place of peace and industry. You men of the north have spoiled that peace, and seem to have no industry in you. I could pass such a sentence on you, my friends, that you would never raise a finger against authority again – but I shall not do that, for I understand a little of what passes through your minds, having been a soldier myself once in my long lifetime, and having known what it is to suffer imprisonment. This time I shall not punish you; but be assured that should you ever give me cause to raise my voice against you again, you will find me to be such a man as will bring terror to your minds whenever you think of me again.'

As the vikings went from the room of Abu Mazur, they saw Marriba playing with her pet leopard in a little alcove. She smiled at them and said softly, 'You are fortunate that I did not tell my father I hated you. If I had done that, who knows what would have happened to you?'

Then she went on playing with the leopard, pulling his tail and tickling his furry ears. The vikings passed by, prodded on by the spear-butts of the guard who escorted them.

When they were again in their quarters, eating rye bread and drinking barley broth, Haro said, 'For that young woman, I would lay down my life. She is the most beautiful creature I have seen.'

Harald said, 'Yes, she is beautiful, but I think she is perhaps cruel too. Did you see how she teased the leopard cub?'

Haro said, 'I would gladly become a leopard cub and be teased by such a princess.'

But Harald only struck him on the back, making him splutter, for his mouth was full of rye bread, and said, 'Take care that Loki is not listening behind the curtains, or you may wake to find yourself a leopard cub in all truth one day!'

Chapter **II** *The Empty Bed*

For three weeks after the fight in the courtyard, the vikings went on quietly and obediently with their work. And
then something happened which led to even stranger
things.

They were being marched to their work in the garden
one day, by their master, Rajik, when they passed by the
prison room in which new slaves were sometimes put
until they grew more accustomed to the idea of servitude.
From the high barred window floated a man's voice,
young and strong and full of an infinite yearning. The
vikings stopped dead and listened, for it was a voice which
spoke their own tongue. And the song it sang was this:

> 'I have sailed in the northern seas,
> Taking the Whale's Way,
> Over the Gannet's Bath,
> Among the ice-capped breakers;
> Song-drunk and drifting,
> Over the lift and the drop of green waters,
> Into the sun's eye, into the West.'

Radbard's eyes filled with tears and his lips trembled
when he spoke. 'That is a northman,' he said. 'A sea-
rover – a sea-bird whose long wings are clipped.'

Haro bit his lip thoughtfully and said, 'He is young
and will feel the pain of imprisonment. But perhaps in a

day or two he will see sense. He will see that a man could be in worse places than this.'

Radbard Crookleg clenched his fists and shut his eyes. 'For some of us,' he said, 'death itself would be better than slavery.' Harald said slowly, 'I am as true a sea-rover as any man, but what good does it do a man to pour out his soul like that, into the foreign air where there is no one to help him?'

They had forgotten Rajik, who had stood aside while they spoke, smiling softly to himself. Suddenly he came forward and whispered, 'Who says there is no one to help a sea-rover who wishes to break from his cage? Who says that a man might not get away from this house, if only he had the right friend to help him?'

Radbard turned and stared at Rajik, who shrugged his shoulders and then continued to walk towards the courtyard. They followed him, for now the song had finished and all was silent in the high prison.

Rajik said nothing more that morning, but often seemed to fix his eyes on Radbard especially, as though he expected the man to open the conversation again. Harald and Haro watched their companion closely, for he appeared to be moody now, and when they met again in the eating hall, they saw that Radbard had taken a bench near to Rajik and was talking excitedly and in a low tone to him. Rajik was replying quietly, glancing over his shoulder many times as he spoke.

Haro said to Harald, 'There is a bird that will fly before long, unless I am mistaken.'

That evening, Harald put his hand on Radbard's shoulder and said, 'Friend, we have been together for a long while. Let us stay together now, for the time may come when we shall find a way towards the north again.'

Radbard stared at him like a man in a dream and said, 'Let us stay together, yes. Let us all go north together now.'

Harald turned away from him and said to Haro, 'He speaks like a man who has drunk some drug and does not understand.'

Haro shook his head and said, 'I fear that Radbard's mind is clouded, Harald. I have seen northmen grow like this before when they have been locked up too long. Their senses leave them and they beat their brains out on stone walls, like a bird trying to fight its way out of a cage.'

They decided that they must keep a watchful eye on their companion from that time onwards, and if possible prevent him from talking too much with Rajik, whose conversation seemed to trouble him.

Two nights later Harald woke from a frightening dream in which he was chained down in a cave on the seashore. As the green tides flowed higher and higher into the cave, Harald saw a large basking shark which tried to get to him. He shouted at the creature in his dream, telling it to beware for he had his father's sword by his side – though even as he dreamed these words, he knew that his hands were tied and that he could not defend himself if the tide rose so high that the shark could get to him. It was at this moment, when the breakers were already rolling over his body, that he woke up with a great start and sat up, mopping his forehead with his hand.

He looked about him, to make sure that he was not in the cave, and then he saw that Radbard was not lying beside him as he usually did. The coverlet was flung back from his pallet of straw and Radbard was not to be seen in the long dormitory room.

Harald touched Haro lightly on the face and woke him. 'Our sea-bird has flown, it seems,' he said. 'Come, we must find him before he runs himself into mortal danger.'

Swiftly the two men rose, passing between the beds of the other slaves and through the open door, where their guard snored at his post, his helmet on the floor beside him, and so out into the long corridor.

The moonlight glimmered onto them as they passed between the pillars of the cloistered passage-way, and at length they ran through the nearest courtyard and so into another passage-way, this time shut off from the light.

Once more they moved silently past a sleeping sentry and as they rounded the next corner, saw a white figure disappearing under an archway.

'That may be Radbard,' whispered Harald, as they ran.

'It looks more like a woman than a man, for it is dressed in long white robes,' said Haro. 'Yet we must make sure.'

Once as they ran a sentry stretched his arms and yawned, and the two men were compelled to draw aside into a little alcove until the soldier had grunted and settled himself to sleep again. Then they passed on, through the great courtyard where they worked each day, and into a square, high-ceilinged chamber.

It was there that they almost ran into the figure in white, for it had stopped and was bending over someone who lay on the floor.

Harald saw immediately that it was Radbard whom

they had pursued, though he was dressed Moorish fashion, his face half-enshrouded by a hood, his waist encircled by a broad black sash.

They came beside him and touched him on the shoulder. He turned to them a face contorted with horror, and pointed to the body on the floor. They bent over the man, and saw that it was Clothair. He was dead. A dagger had been driven into his back, between the joints of his body armour. Harald bent and looked at the weapon; it had a long, red-leather hilt.

Then he looked at the empty scabbard that swung from the black sash at Radbard's waist. 'Did you kill Clothair?' asked Harald, striving to keep the horrified disgust from his voice.

But Radbard only shook his head, helplessly. 'He was dead when I stumbled over his body a moment ago. I had no dagger. This robe and scabbard were left for me by Rajik, who showed me how I could escape this night when all the guards were drugged.'

Haro said grimly, 'Then friend Rajik has tricked you, Radbard. For now suspicion will fall on you and if they catch you, your end is certain.'

Radbard said simply, 'Rajik always hated Clothair, he even told me so. Well, what shall be, shall be; there is nothing more to say.'

He stood in the glimmer of moonlight like a man in a drugged sleep, hardly able to care for himself.

It was then that Harald's sharp ears caught the sound of shuffling footsteps along a far passageway. He signed to the others to be still and said, 'There are men at the end of that passageway. Where does it lead?'

Radbard said, 'That is the way to the treasure chamber. Rajik showed it to me only yesterday.'

'Then that is where we shall find him, and take our vengeance on him,' said Harald, suddenly angry with a cold and fearsome anger.

Chapter 12 *The Vengeance of Abu Mazur*

At the corner of the passageway, the three vikings halted. Before them, in the semi-darkness, a group of figures moved slowly and quietly, as though they were engaged in some arduous task. Harald's keen eyes picked out five figures, dressed after the manner of the house-guards, and led, it seemed by a small crooked man – Rajik the gardener.

'They are armed,' he whispered to Haro, 'for I see the glint of sword blades.'

'One of us carries a weapon, too,' said Haro ironically, holding out his hand. Harald saw that he had taken the red-hilted dagger which had killed their friend, Clothair.

It was then that they heard Rajik's unmistakable voice.

'Go quietly, my comrades,' he said, 'for soon we shall come out into the great chamber, and then we may need to have our wits about us!'

Almost as by instinct, Harald leapt forward, crying, 'Your wits will not save you now, Rajik the serpent! You have murdered Clothair and tricked our brother, Radbard! Now you would rob your master!'

There was a frightened cry in the gloom of the passageway, then muffled oaths and words of anger, as the robbers realized that they were assailed not by the guards of the house, but by three slaves.

There was the sound of boxes being flung to the ground hurriedly, then the vikings were among the robbers, grappling with them before they could bring their swords into action.

In the half-darkness, it was impossible for the vikings to fight with the skill which was theirs by day, but they gave a good account of themselves. Radbard was the first to speak, after the battle had started. His comrades heard him say, 'And that is for you, Snake Rajik, and for Clothair who was a good friend to us in his way!'

They heard Rajik's high voice call out for mercy, and then a groan took the place of his crying and he fell.

Haro was fighting like a berserk now, holding two men at bay with his long-bladed dagger, and driving them back down the passageway, towards the treasure chamber.

Harald had grappled his opponent round the waist and was slowly bending him back, when he felt a sharp pain in his side and then knew that he had been wounded and could exert his great strength no longer. 'To me, Radbard,' he called hoarsely. 'I am hurt and cannot hold this one much longer!'

A great blackness, blacker than the night itself, swept over Harald's eyes, and as he heard Radbard's feet shuffling towards him, he fell, unable to hold the enemy at bay any further.

Radbard reached forward and took Harald's opponent by the hair of his head and dragged him forward, and even as Radbard struck the man at the nape of the neck with his hard clenched fist, a great light shone on them from the high chamber, and Abu Mazur stood there, surrounded by a dozen guards, the torchlight glinting on their helmets and poised javelins.

The fight in the passageway ceased, suddenly, as a thunderstorm when the sun breaks out again and the air is still.

Then, in the great hall, Abu Mazur sat in judgement, the fighters standing or lying before his gilded chair, the guards standing in a circle about them, fierce in the flaring torchlight.

'What has any man to say before I speak?' the master asked, turning his eagle's eyes upon them all in turn.

Rajik, still shaken by the great blow which Radbard had dealt him, flung himself before the gilded chair and held out his hands in supplication.

'Listen to me, master,' he said. 'I am your good servant and have always served you faithfully. Tonight I heard strange sounds and came here to find these three vikings dragging your treasure from its resting-place.'

Abu Mazur nodded and said, 'Who are these men who were fighting with the vikings? I have not seen them before.'

Rajik said, 'They are good true men of the town, of Jebel Tarik, old friends of mine. They were drinking with me, as friends do, in my little room that you let me have, in your graciousness of heart.'

'And who killed Clothair?' asked Abu Mazur, gently, for he had always trusted the Frank and was sad to see him lying dead before him.

Rajik pointed an accusing finger at Radbard. 'That one did it. He struck him down with the dagger which lies before you now.'

Abu regarded him steadily for a moment and then said, 'The thing which lies before me is called Rajik – for Rajik killed Clothair, and Rajik brought in these murderers to steal his master's treasure.'

The gardener began to protest, but Abu Mazur waved him to silence.

'Have no doubts, Rajik, I was well aware that you were plotting against me. After all, I must keep my spies like any other rich merchant in these troubled times. And I know these friends of yours. That one is Rajam the Sheep-stealer – his father was hanged last year in Africa; that is Bela Tok, who killed a shepherd outside Granada three weeks ago; and the others, who are dead or unconscious, I do not care which, are also known to me.'

Rajik gazed at him in bewilderment. 'But, master, you said you had never seen them before.'

Abu Mazur passed a weary hand over his forehead and said, 'No, I have not seen them, but my spies bring me accurate descriptions, you dullard. I have eyes in my mind, too, friend Rajik, which is something you have not – nor will you live to have now.'

At this, Haro, although wounded deeply in the neck, gave a great shout of laughter and clapped the wretched Rajik on the back, almost knocking him flying. 'There,' he said, 'but it takes a big wolf to catch a little wolf! Friend Rajik, you are nicely in the trap now. Let us see you wriggle clear this time!'

At this the guards would have silenced Haro, but Abu held up his hand, ordering them to let the viking be.

Then he addressed them, saying, 'My rough northern friends, for now I believe you are my friends, I am grateful to you. You shall not find me a forgetful master, and from this time your lives may perhaps be sweeter. Your chieftain, who lies wounded before me, shall have Cloth-air's place in my household and you shall help him in his task. Who knows, perhaps one day you may become my guards.'

Then he gave orders that Harald should be carried carefully to the physician, Malabar el Arrash, who lived in the house, to be treated for the sword-cut which had pierced deeply into his right side.

As the vikings rose and followed the guards who carried their friend, they heard the voice of Abu Mazur once more speaking to Rajik and the robbers who had tried to steal the treasure.

'As for you,' it said, 'your traitorous eyes shall not see another dawn. You shall die where you stand now, and your fate shall be a lasting warning to any others who think to gain easily by night what I have spent many hard days in getting.'

Radbard said, 'He deserves his fate, for he would have brought it upon me, but for your friendship, my brother.'

After that, they did not mention Rajik, the little gardener-man, again. Nor did they ever walk through that echoing hall where the sentence had been passed.

Haro's neck soon healed, but spring had turned to summer before Harald was well, nor would he have walked again had not the great skill of Malabar el Arrash been devoted to its full on his behalf.

But now, as the first heavy heat of the summer sun began to beat down, already almost unbearably, on the city of Jebel Tarik, the three vikings sat once more on the white terrace overlooking the steaming harbour.

The two others were teasing Harald, for he was wearing his helmet and armour for the first time since he had been appointed to fill Clothair's position.

'Why did you not let them cut your hair, King Harald?' asked Radbard, mischievously, for he had now regained something of his old spirits. 'Your helmet does not fit properly. It was made for a man with short hair.'

Harald said, 'No man shall cut my hair, friend Baldhead! I would rather have my own hair than any helmet!'

This annoyed Radbard, who was going very thin on top, and he immediately began to grapple with Harald, trying to roll him on the ground.

Then suddenly Haro began to whistle, warning them that someone was coming, but it was too late. Marriba stood behind them, smiling, her leopard cub on a golden chain at her side.

'What a pretty picture, Captain Harald,' she said, 'to

see a great warrior rolling on the floor like a little boy.'

Harald looked up sheepishly and then, unable to say anything, took an apple from his leather pouch and flung it into the air. The girl watched it go, wondering, and then saw Harald rise to his feet, pull out his sword with one swift motion, and, as the apple came down at arm's height, cut it through downwards and then, almost with the same movement, across, so that the fruit fell in four even parts at her feet.

The look of amazement on the girl's face was such that the three vikings burst into a roar of laughter.

Haro said, 'He is a show-off, is this Harald, Princess. Look, if he will give me his sword, I will show you one even better than that.'

Marriba said slyly, 'You are still a slave, Haro Roughneck. You are not allowed to have a sword, like Harald.'

Harald said, 'I am the Captain here, my lady, not you. If I give him a sword, that is my affair.'

But although he spoke abruptly, it was not through anger, but to cover his embarrassment that a girl should have seen him wrestling like a little boy on the ground. Then he handed his sword to Haro, who took three figs from his pocket and, having disposed them evenly in his left hand, flung them all into the air at once. As they came down in the sunlight, he struck at each one, neatly and quickly, with blows like those which a cat gives to a rolling ball of wool. The three figs lay on the white marble pavement, equally divided. Haro tossed the sword back to Harald, who caught it.

'Not a bad sword,' said Haro, carelessly, 'though I like one a little heavier in the blade. That is a lady's toy.'

Laughing, the girl turned to Radbard and said, 'After that is there anything you dare do, Crookleg?'

Radbard scratched his nose for a while and then said slyly, 'Yes, but it has nothing to do with swords, my lady.'

'So much the better,' said the girl, 'for this cutting and carving becomes tedious after a time. Well, what can you show me?'

Radbard simply said, 'This, and no more!'

He turned suddenly and snatched up a handful of pebbles from the edge of the steps. A large black carrion crow was sitting on the red roof, at the edge of the platform. Swiftly Radbard threw at the bird, which seemed to expect something of the sort and was ready to fly away. The first pebble struck the bird on the body and toppled it down the roof, but it rose again and was almost away when the viking threw again. This stone brought the bird back to the eaves, fluttering. Radbard raised his hand to throw the third pebble, but Marriba held his arm.

'That is enough, barbarian,' she said. 'I do not love those birds, but I will not have you kill one just to show me your skill at throwing pebbles.'

Radbard shrugged his shoulders, and the bird, glad of the respite, gathered itself and flew away over the house, crying hoarsely.

'All the same,' said Marriba, when it had gone, 'I have never seen such marksmanship before in my life. A man like you does not need a sword, Radbard Crookleg, when there are stones about to throw!'

With that she went away, and Haro watched her go, sighing and holding his hand to his heart. The other two then rolled him on the ground, telling him that he was a dolt and a love-sick clown.

That afternoon a messenger came to fetch them into the presence of Abu Mazur, who met them with a grave face.

Radbard whispered, 'I know what it is, she has reported me for throwing at that bird, and now we are all to be punished.'

But it was not that at all.

Abu Mazur allowed them to sit down, a privilege which amazed them, and then said to them slowly, 'My friends, my dear daughter, Marriba, is not well. Her delicate constitution was not intended by nature for the heavy heat of this city and I am afraid that if she stays with me in the house here through the summer, she may come to harm. My good doctor, Malabar el Arrash, of whose skill you already know a little, tells me that my daughter must go to a more northerly climate, away from this heat, if she is to retain her health and happiness.'

Radbard said absently, 'Along the fjords now they will be sailing in their boats with the red and white sails, and already men will have returned to the villages with stores of treasure . . .'

Abu Mazur's sharp eyes silenced him in his dreaming. 'I do not speak of the far north, my friend,' he said sternly. 'That is a place where only bears and wolves live. It is not a place for such a frail flower as Marriba. Remember that.'

There was a silence then, and Abu Mazur rubbed his chin thoughtfully. At last he spoke to Harald alone, ignoring the others.

'I trust you, northman, and so does my daughter. In recent weeks I have come to believe that I trust you more than I do any of my servants, of whatever race or quality. If I gave you charge of the fast ship which is to take my daughter to the northern islands, what would you say?'

Harald fell to his knees on the floor and said earnestly, 'I should thank you most deeply, Abu Mazur. I can say no more.'

Abu Mazur said quickly, 'I should not ask for any more, northman, except that I should require you all to kneel before me, and putting your hands within mine, swear on your honour that you would obey my daughter in all things and would never question her judgement.'

The three men kneeled before Abu Mazur and took that oath.

With a wry smile he said gently, 'It is my right and my duty to convert men such as you to the true faith, to Allah, but I am not always strict in these matters for even good men vary so much in their beliefs. If you were of my faith, I would ask you to swear on the Beard of the Prophet, perhaps, and that would be binding; but I ask you to swear on your honour as fightingmen of the north, and I know that you will not betray me.'

Haro said swiftly, 'May Odin's ravens peck out my heart if I disobey your daughter in anything she commands, be it great or small, for I would willingly die for her.'

Abu Mazur touched him gently on the shoulder and said, 'You are a good man, though a fool in many ways, northman. Take my daughter to her relatives in the islands, where the air is fresh and sea-borne, and the sun strikes less shrewdly, and when you return with her at the fall of leaf, you shall all be made freedmen, to go or to stay here as you wish.'

Then he clapped his hands as a sign that the audience was ended and the three vikings walked down the long arcades, unable to speak for the joy that was in their hearts to be going in a ship once again.

Marriba watched them from her window grille and smiled, though when her father came into her room to tell her the result of the meeting, she lay back in her bed again and put her hand over her eyes.

'Oh, father,' she said, 'the heat is so oppressive. I can hardly stand it. I shall die, I know I shall die.'

Abu Mazur bent and stroked her head lightly. 'Patience, my lamb, patience my chicken,' he said soothingly. 'In two days from now you will be on the seas with our brave vikings to look after you. Then your spirits will rise again and you will be my lovely daughter once more.'

Marriba shrugged petulantly and said, 'No, I shall not! I shall die, I tell you, father, and then you will be sorry for bringing me here to Jebel Tarik where the wind is as hot as a furnace and the stones burn one to touch them.'

Her father tip-toed sorrowfully from the room to fetch the physician, but as soon as the door curtain had swung to, Marriba jumped from her bed and ran to the window grille, to see if the vikings were still in sight.

But they were not; now they stood looking over the harbour wall at a low and rakish vessel with a triangular sail of red and gold.

'Ten oar ports and a steerboard like one of our own longships,' said Harald, pointing.

Haro gazed in silence at the high sharp prow and the bright steel grappling hooks. A great lump had risen in his throat and he was afraid of crying if he tried to answer.

Suddenly Radbard began to shout and dance and cry, all at the same time. 'By Odin,' he said, 'a ship! A ship! A ship!'

Then, with the tears streaming down their cheeks, they began to hug each other like clumsy bears.

Part Three

One day out from Jebel Tarik, Harald stood at the helm, holding a north-easterly course through the torpid blue waters of the Middle Sea. Once more he felt the salt upon his face and his heart rejoiced. Radbard and Haro stood in the prow, pointing excitedly at this and that – a white gull swooping low over the water, a brightly-coloured sail on a distant ship, anything.

Marriba sat under an awning aft, stroking her leopard cub and sometimes deigning to speak to the old woman, her personal slave, who accompanied her. This old woman, Lalla, was a devout creature, for ever at her prayers, and hating the whole idea of a voyage, even though Marriba told her again and again that they could come to no harm, with the vikings to guard them, and ten fierce Syrian oarsmen, who were as able with a sword as with an oar or a sail. But still the old woman shook her head mournfully and wept that she had ever come to this . . .

Sometimes Marriba strummed on a golden lute that her father had given her as a parting present, and then the sweet music seemed to echo in time to the beat of the oars and the cry of the sea-birds, and all seemed gay in the sunshine.

Often they passed other ships belonging to Marriba's father, which always gave a loud call on their trumpets to show that they recognized their master's fast ship and were paying their respects to it.

Harald was thinking how beautiful Jebel Tarik had looked, as they sailed away a day ago, set in terraces on the high rock, white and red and yellow in the morning sunshine. It had quite gone from his mind that he had ever been a slave there, and now when he looked back, it seemed a place of good fortune – in spite of the fact that to get there, he had lost many friends, a ship, and a load of treasure.

His thoughts swung back to his comrades – Haro, Goff, Sven and the others ... yes, even the giant Grummoch, who had looked like becoming a true sea-rover and then had jumped into the water and put an end to himself rather than be taken by the Arab pirates ... What a shame it was, thought Harald, that one lost one's ship-mates! And how glorious it would be to sail with all the good men one had ever known, in the biggest longship of all time, to the west, to the west, to the west...

But now he was sailing to the north-east, he reflected, half-sadly for the moment, and he knew only two men in this fast little ship.

He was roused from his day-dream by a blast on the silver whistle, which Marriba used to call her shipmaster to her, on her father's orders.

Harald beckoned to Radbard, who ran aft and took the helm. Then he made his way to the girl as she sat under the striped awning.

Marriba smiled at him and indicated a cushion at her feet with a motion of her hand.

'Sit down, shipmaster,' she said, gently. 'There is something I wish to say to you, now that we are over a day at sea.'

Harald still stood, feeling that he should not show any familiarity with his master's daughter; but Marriba pointed to the cushion again, this time imperiously. 'Remember, you swore to obey me in all things – yes, in all things, Captain,' she said, smiling.

Harald frowned and said, 'What shall be, shall be. What is it that troubles you, lady Marriba, then?'

Marriba smiled sweetly at him and said, 'Nothing troubles me, Captain; and nothing is going to trouble me, either. You will obey all my commands, and then nothing will trouble me. Is that clear?'

Harald nodded, puzzled. 'Yes,' he said, 'I shall obey you in all reasonable things.'

Marriba said sternly, 'You will obey me in all things – reasonable or otherwise, Captain. For that is the oath you took to my father, and that is the oath he will expect you to keep.'

Harald said, 'Yes, but if you ordered me to run this fine ship on to a rock, not even my oath would make me –'

Marriba stopped him with a wave of her hand.

'I should not do anything so stupid,' she said quietly, 'for we need this ship to take us to Byzantium, don't we, Captain?'

Harald jumped to his feet. 'What do you mean, Byzantium?' he said, in amazement.

'Just that, Captain,' said Marriba, fingering the silky ears of her leopard cub. 'I am ordering you to change course, and to set this ship's nose towards Byzantium, or

Miklagard as you barbarians call it, towards the Empire itself. Is that clear?'

Harald said thickly, 'No, it is not clear. I am to take you to the northern islands, a day and a half away, to pass the summer there with relatives who expect you.'

Marriba sighed and said, 'How dull you northmen are. A man of the south would have seen my point immediately. Well, if you must know, my dear relatives in the northern islands will wait for me in vain. They are old and dull and would be no fun for a young girl like me to pass the summer with. I am going to pass the summer, and longer than the summer, with someone more to my liking, dear Captain.'

Harald gazed at her with wide-open eyes.

'You know someone in Byzantium?' he said slowly.

Marriba mimicked his slow speech. 'Yes, dear Captain,' she said. 'I know a Prince there, a Roman, who wishes to marry me. Is that clear?'

Harald stood back a pace and rubbed his forehead.

'But does your father know about this?' he said.

Marriba smiled wickedly and answered, 'No, dear Captain, he does not; and who is there to bother him with such news? You will take me to my Prince in Byzantium, it is an old arrangement with us, and then everyone will be happy.'

Harald said, 'But what if I refuse?'

Someone had stepped behind him. It was Haro. He put his hand firmly on Harald's shoulder and said, 'You will not refuse what this lady asks you. You have sworn an oath, as I have, and you will obey her.'

Harald looked into Haro's eyes and saw that he was deadly serious.

'You are bemused with this young woman, Haro,' said the shipmaster. 'Abu Mazur didn't mean us to obey her in things like this.'

Haro answered calmly, 'Who are you to decide what Abu Mazur meant? Do your duty as a Captain, Harald. And if I am bemused with her, well and good, that is no crime. I shall see her delivered safely to her Prince if it is the last thing I do.'

Radbard met Harald outside the awning and said, 'I have heard what has been said.'

Harald said, 'You must be the final judge, Radbard. What do you say?'

Radbard Crookleg scratched his long nose and then smiled at Marriba over Harald's shoulder.

'I have always wanted to see Miklagard,' he said.

And before Harald could reply, Radbard had walked back to the helm, to swing the ship round so her prow faced towards the east.

Marriba said nothing, but picked up her golden lute and began to strum lightly.

Harald stumped away to the prow of the ship and stood staring into the white foam that lashed about the bow. But at last even he relented and by evening time sat with the others under the awning, eating and drinking and telling those immensely long tales which all northmen rejoice in.

Excited as they all were, the trials of the many weeks which followed caused Harald to doubt his wisdom in agreeing to the long voyage to Miklagard.

When they drew too close inshore off Tunis, a dhow came out after them, and though they easily outstripped it, yet they lost three Syrian oarsmen in the flight of arrows which followed them.

Marriba said bitterly, 'If my father knew of that, he would have the crew of that dhow strangled with bow-strings.'

Harald retorted, 'If your father knew, he would prob-ably reward them all for trying to recapture his wicked daughter.'

But this only made Marriba laugh and Harald said no more.

Again, they almost ran aground on the coast of Sicily, and were chased by a long warship which got close en-ough to fling out its grappling hooks. Harald swung the helm hard over, almost capsizing the shallow craft, and unseating the oarsmen, who by this time were ready to surrender to anyone who looked fiercely enough at them; but they got free again, and put in at Malta to replenish their food and water, which had only been sufficient to take them to the Balearic Islands in the first place.

At Malta, yet another misfortune befell them, which made Harald feel that the hand of Odin was turned against them on this voyage. Wandering in the woods above the shore, while the water-skins were being filled, Radbard trod upon a viper and was bitten deeply in the ankle. He struck off the creature's head and then tried to let out the poison from the wound with his sword. Harald and Haro found him, hours later, staggering about in the woods, his eyes wild, and babbling that he must get back to the fjord to plant the barley seeds for his old mother.

Harald examined their comrade's leg. It was very swollen and had red streaks running up it towards his body.

'There is nothing we can do, friend,' said Haro, when he saw this. 'Radbard has run his course. It is the will of Odin.'

Later they fetched the old woman, Lalla, who was skilled in herbal medicines. She clucked her tongue against the roof of her mouth and said that if they had been back home, she would have known just where to find the right herb to cure this snake sting – but here, ah no, it was impossible. Allah wanted this man, she said, and it would be wicked to keep Allah and Radbard apart.

As she said this, Radbard's mind seemed to clear for a moment or two and he even smiled grimly at the old woman.

'Be assured, old one,' he said, 'it is Odin who requests the pleasure of my company at his feast, not Allah! And I am ready to go.'

Harald was holding him at the time, and felt Radbard's

head suddenly go slack on his shoulders. He laid the man down gently and then they covered him with boughs and turf, for the wood there was too green and damp to make a funeral pyre.

On the way to the ship, Harald dried the tears on his cheeks and said, 'Haro, my only friend, this is a bad voyage. But I swear to you that I shall make Miklagard pay for this. I shall leave that city as rich as a Prince, or shall die there !'

Haro did not answer and they went back to the ship in silence.

When they got aboard, Harald solemnly handed Radbard's sword to Marriba. 'Here, lady,' he said with a quiet bitterness, 'this is a present from the man you have killed by your wilfulness.'

He was sorry he had said this when Marriba suddenly burst into tears. But after that, she regarded Harald very oddly, at times, as though she wished to punish him for his words to her that day.

Then their luck seemed to change without warning. A week later they ran in north of Crete, to be met by a large Roman man-of-war that stood high out of the water. There was no escaping this time, and indeed Harald had little heart to try that trick again. He merely ordered the rowers to leave their oars and get out their swords. Then he walked to the prow and stood waiting for the first men to come at him.

The Roman ship flung out a grappling hook and drew the other ship alongside. Three officers, splendid in golden armour, jumped lightly down beside Harald, their swords rattling in their scabbards.

'What cargo do you carry?' the first man asked in Arabic.

Harald said, 'A woman, nothing more.' He was weary of the whole voyage and would almost have surrendered Marriba at that moment, so annoyed was he at the loss of Radbard.

The officers strode down between the Syrian rowers to the awning where Marriba sat, putting on a brave face, twitching the strings of her lute, as though she were accustomed to such situations every day.

When they reached her, they bowed and smiled courteously.

'On what errand do you travel, lady?' said their leader.

Marriba smiled up at him and whispered something which he had to bend to hear, her voice had suddenly gone so weak.

To Harald's great surprise, the officer bowed again and said for all to hear, 'A thousand pardons, lady. If I had known, I would not have put you to the indignity of answering my questions.'

As he spoke, the other two officers knelt before Marriba, their heads bowed low.

Haro nudged Harald and whispered, 'If they do not take care, they will break their long noses on the deck boards!'

Then the officer spoke again and said, 'The times are dangerous ones, Your Highness, and our Emperor Constantine, your beloved, would think ill of us if we allowed you to travel further without our escort. Indeed, great lady, if I confess the truth, we have been watching for you these three months, up and down the islands, for your message that you would find some occasion to travel east before the summer was out pleased the Emperor Constantine greatly.'

Harald hissed, 'To think that all the time she was planning this trick! I will never trust womankind again!'

Even Haro looked a trifle put out as he heard the officer's words.

When these men had gone, with many bows and a great swirl of their purple cloaks, Marriba beckoned to Harald and said slyly to him, 'So now you know, great Captain! I am to be betrothed to the Emperor in Constantinople. Are you not glad that you did not disobey me now, when I ordered you to sail here?'

Harald said angrily, 'What would your good father say to such a match? You are a Muslim and this emperor is no doubt a Christian, of some sort.'

Marriba said quietly, 'Be assured, friend northman, he is a very great Christian; one of the greatest! And so shall I become, in due course, for there are some trifling obstacles to be cleared away, I understand. First this lover of mine is already betrothed to one Rotrud, no doubt an ugly creature, the daughter of that Frankish king Charles, who lets himself be called "The Great".'

Even Harald gasped at her insolence, for he and his folk had good reason to fear the name of Charlemagne.

'And what is the other obstacle, O Powerful Queen?' he asked, in as bitter a tone as he dared.

Marriba examined the nails of her right hand negligently and at last said, 'My Constantine's mother, Irene, a woman of Athens and no true Roman, seems bent on making trouble. I gather that she hopes to rule here herself, and so did not take the oath of fealty to her son. But we shall attend to that matter when I am installed in Byzantium, friend Harald, that we shall! Then there will be no obstacle.'

Harald said slowly, 'No, no obstacle then, my lady. And how old is this Emperor of yours?'

Marriba struck three light chords on her lute before she answered, and then she did so with a defiant expression on her ivory face.

'He is fifteen, great Captain,' she said. 'But fifteen in a brave warrior is the match of twenty in, say, a mere seaman, shipmaster!'

Harald stared at her aghast; then he controlled himself and strode to the prow of his ship to supervise the loading of certain delicacies which the officers on the warship had decided it was wise to offer to the beautiful young lady who had come so far to marry their Emperor. Not that they were afraid of her or of him, but it was as well to keep in favour – with both sides if possible – and in any case they would report all they knew, as soon as they landed, to the Lady Irene, the Emperor's rather overbearing mother, from whom they drew a second salary, after the little Emperor had paid them off with his miserable pittance.

On their high deck they looked down onto the fast ship of Abu Mazur. Their Captain, the one with the hooked nose and the curly black hair, who had spoken to Marriba so respectfully, said to his two lieutenants, 'Well, gentlemen, the situation grows more and more amusing! He sends us to meet her and guard her to the port; she sends us to capture her and, if possible, to drown her quietly, off whichever of the islands is the most convenient! Which shall we do, gentlemen?'

The two lieutenants grinned at each other, admiring their reflections in each other's armour. Then the elder of them turned, twirled his long black moustaches and said silkily, 'Let us take her back safely, my Captain. It would be more amusing – I should love to see what old Irene says when this young Arab lass begins to queen it over her in the Court!'

'Done!' said the Captain, slapping the other quite gently on the back. 'So that is settled! She lives, for the time being! And now we will go below decks and drink some of that sweet white wine I had brought on board this morning. It looks superb, gentlemen, quite superb! Far too good for the likes of poor soldiers like us!'

They went below laughing gaily. Harald watched them from his ship and wondered what had pleased them so hugely. It was perhaps just as well that he did not know.

Chapter **16** *Miklagard*

Three days later the two ships had passed between the many islands and had reached the Sea of Marmara, had skirted the Golden Gate and were running into an anchorage but a stone's throw from the great golden-roofed Palace of Justinian.

Though the heat beat down unmercifully, to be reflected from the oily water, Marriba had decked herself out in a robe and cloak of heavy silk, and had braided her raven-black hair with thick pieces of corded ribbon, shot through and through with strands of gold and silver thread.

She stood upon the deck, among the rowers, gazing in wonder at the many glories of this Miklagard to which they had come, the Jewel of the World.

Beyond the battlemented walls, set round with dark cypress-trees, rose tier after tier of roofs, some red, some green, some golden, surmounted again by immense domes, that glistened gloriously in the sunshine, and great arches supported by twisted columns of marble; and over these yet again, high towers and minarets, that seemed to reach up through the deep blue sky to heaven itself. The vikings saw the immense aqueducts which spanned the vast city like many-legged monsters of white stone and pointed in awe.

'Aiee!' gasped Haro, 'but they are impossible! No man

could put stone on stone to grow so high up towards the clouds! I shall never believe it! And when I leave this place, I shall know that it was all a dream!'

Harald laughed at him and said, 'If ever you leave it, friend!'

And everywhere they looked, there was such magnificence; northward, across the Golden Horn, was the suburb, Pera, two miles away, its layers of white houses rising up from the blue waters towards the bluer sky, like some fantastic betrothal cake, set with olive trees; and eastward, a mile across the Bosporus, lay Chrysopolis, purple-roofed and splendid above the water, its harbour gay with the many-coloured sails that bobbed lazily on the swell.

Harald grinned and said, 'And do you recall, Haro, that when we first looked down on King MacMiorog's cattle ranch, we said that it must surely rival Miklagard!'

Haro nodded and said, 'It was to this place what a ladybird is to a stallion!'

Then the many trumpets blew and at the signal the two ships pulled into the white-stoned harbour.

'Look, look!' said Marriba, excitedly, 'in that litter with the purple canopy decorated with silver! That is the Emperor, he has come to meet me! Oh, look!'

Harald and Haro nudged each other and stood aside to let the girl go forward on to the plank. The three officers from the war vessel waited on the harbour to lead her to the Emperor Constantine.

Harald and Haro followed at a respectful distance, staring about them at the many soldiers, all in their golden armour and red cloaks, or draped in long purple vestments as they sat on their motionless white horses, their black helmet plumes nodding in the morning breeze that blew down, soft and odorous, from the high city.

Marriba stood before the litter, which was carried by four great Negro slaves. She seemed irresolute and nervous, as though now that she had reached Byzantium, she wished she could be back in the safety of her father's house at Jebel Tarik, where she was the most important person . . .

Then the curtains of the litter were drawn aside and the Emperor slowly got down on to the red carpet which had been spread on the harbour stones.

Haro's eyes grew wide and his mouth fell open.

'What!' he gasped. 'Can that be the Great One we have come so far to meet!'

Constantine was a weak and sickly child, there was no gainsaying it. His thin fair hair hung lankly down his pale face; his light-blue eyes seemed faded and almost colourless; his small red mouth was as petulant as a baby's. And not all the bright, tall diadems, the robes and cloaks, stiff with fine metals and jewels, could make him look other than what he was.

'Poor little puppet!' said Harald, under his breath.

'I would rather be a shepherd lad along the fjords than this pretty doll,' said Haro, in contempt.

The many officers bowed low before the Emperor, and even Marriba knelt on the stones, for the red carpet did not reach as far as the spot where she was made to stand.

The Emperor Constantine looked down at her

haughtily, his heavy-lidded eyes half-closed. Then he extended his thin pale hand, heavy with pretty rings, and speaking in a high voice, bade her stand by him.

When she had done this, he looked past her and said slowly, 'Where are the brave men who brought you to Byzantium? Where are the men who stole you away from your father to bring you to me?'

Marriba was about to speak when the senior officer said, 'Most High, there are the Syrian rowers, still sitting in the ship.'

The Emperor waved his white hand languidly and said, 'I do not mean the rowers. Their work is finished now. I give them the ship they sit in for their pains. They may go when they will and row away, wherever they please. That is all one to me. I ask who was the captain of that ship, the one to whom thanks must be given for this lady's safe passage here.'

The officer turned and beckoned to Harald and Haro to step nearer the Emperor.

'These are the men, both northmen, Most High,' he said.

The Emperor Constantine gazed at them for a moment or two, his petty mouth half-smiling. Then he said abruptly, 'Those who know how to steal such a lady from her father might one day know the way to steal her away from me. That must not be. Take these men to a place where they will steal nothing else. What is done to them there, to prevent them from harming any other man, I care not.'

While the vikings were still numb with the shock of this command, many soldiers closed in on them from every side, and they felt their arms being dragged behind them and pinioned.

Harald shouted out, 'Lady Marriba, help us! We served you well!'

But a soldier clapped his hand over Harald's mouth, and he could say no more.

Marriba did not look at him. Her head was bowed and she did not seem to see what was happening. Then, struggling as violently as they could, the vikings were dragged away from the harbour.

Chapter 17 *The Challenge*

The admiration with which the two vikings had first greeted Miklagard had now turned to disgust and even hatred. The narrow cell in which they had spent their last three days was dank and stinking; its earthen floor was covered with a mess of rotting rushes; the only light came down to them from a window set high in the wall, and level with the pavement of the street outside, for this cell was partly an underground structure.

Twice a day, a sour-faced gaoler thrust two flat pannikins into the cell; the one containing a mixture of broken rye bread, pieces of cold meat, and grease-scummed gravy; the other filled to the brim with water, which, more often than not, was cloudy and of a rusty-brown colour. Always it was brackish and next to undrinkable.

The vikings complained loudly, but the gaoler ignored them and went away after he had pushed the repulsive food at them.

There was one other occupant of this cell, a bent and wizened old man, dressed in a single garment of rough sacking. His hair was quite white and his eyes sightless. When he heard them complaining, he said haltingly, in a dialect which was a mixture of Arabic and Greek, 'This food is not so bad; it has kept me alive for twenty years! Be thankful that they left you your eyes to find the food when the gaoler brings it in. They were not so kind to me, my friends.'

The vikings wondered about the terrible nature of the crime for which the old man had been so punished, but one day he told them that he had once been a Chancellor in the court, and had been thrown into prison, blinded, in the time of the Emperor Constantine Copronymus, because he would not confess that he had received bribes from certain of the bishops.

Haro said directly, 'And did you receive bribes?'

The old man shook his head and replied, 'No, but that made no difference. They did not believe me. They blinded me in their usual manner, by making me look at a white hot iron held close to my eyes. It has happened to countless people in Byzantium, and will no doubt happen a countless number of times again. You are lucky to have escaped it. It is a distressing thing to happen, especially to a young man, and I was only thirty at the time.'

Harald said bitterly, 'It seems to me that Miklagard is most like a beautiful but cruel woman, nothing better.'

The old man smiled and said, 'I could give it a harsher name, but there, I am old now and must not shorten my days by hatred.'

Haro said, 'But things are changed now, surely; that happened many years ago. Now that there are new monarchs, why do they not let you go free?'

The old man answered, 'They have forgotten me, my friend. One expects no justice in Byzantium, in any case. It is a hard city. And anyway, if they set me free, I should starve, for my family has gone away, and I have nothing. I am content here, that is all. So you see why I do not complain about the food, bad as it is; it keeps life in one's body.'

Another day Harald said to the old man, 'Why do you want to live? This life is a living death, no more.'

The old man shrugged his white head and said, 'No, one lives after a fashion. You see, every other day a little street beggar comes to this window and tells me what is going on in the city, what is happening at the Court, and so on. In that way I live, for I can picture the scenes in my head, as though I had my eyes again; and at night I dream that I am amongst the courtiers again, listening to gossip, meeting the new arrivals at the Court, and such like. Yes, it is a sort of life and I would rather have that than have no life at all.'

Then he went on to tell them many things; that Byzantium was not a happy city; that the taxes were always high, and no justice to be had; that the Court, the Church, and the Judges were all corrupt; that Irene the mother of the Emperor-to-be, hated her son and wished to rule herself over the Eastern Roman Empire.

'She refused to take the oath of fealty to him,' said the old man, 'although all the others did – the provincial governors, the ministers, the senators – even the artisan guilds, the common workers, you know. But not Irene! No, she has already tried to break off the young man's betrothal to the daughter of Charlemagne, in case her son might become too powerful if the marriage took place. And' – here his old voice fell to a whisper – 'they tell me that in a great quarrel with him, in the full Court, some days ago, she even threatened to have him blinded, if he did not mend his ways and obey her in all things.'

Haro blew out his cheeks and said, 'I thought my old mother was strict when she used to thrash me with a broom-handle, but that was the gentlest of love compared with this. No, friends, I would not be a little emperor for all the wealth of Miklagard.'

The old man smiled and said, 'And Miklagard, as you call it, is very wealthy, very rich. I know that from my own experience here. There are treasure houses of the Court situated in many unlikely places throughout the town, and even beyond the town walls. Look, just to show you ...'

He took up a straw and began to sketch out a plan of Miklagard in the soft earth of the floor. Harald and Haro watched, amazed at the old man's detailed knowledge, though he was blind.

'There,' he said, when he had finished. 'I have shown you ten treasure houses. What think you of that? And I know only a little of what must be the final truth.'

The two vikings surveyed the sketch earnestly, letting it bite into their memories like acid on a plate of metal.

'Wonderful,' they said. 'And are you sure that this will not have changed since you have been in this prison?'

The old man shook his head. 'They have never changed, those treasure cells, since Byzantium was founded. They will not change now.'

That night, as they lay trying to get to sleep on the hard floor, Haro whispered to Harald, 'If ever we do get free, I know one way of getting our revenge on that little puppet of an Emperor!'

'So do I, my friend,' said Harald. 'But how should we carry it away with us?'

Haro whispered, 'Let us cross that bridge when we come to it, shipmaster! First catch the pig before you eat him!'

The next day they evolved a plan of escape, though when they told the old man, he only laughed and said that it would never work. All the same, they determined to see what would happen.

So Harald climbed on to Haro's shoulders and when the passers-by became most numerous, began to call out in his rough Arabic, 'There is not a man in Byzantium I would not fight! Not one I would not meet, with my right hand tied behind me! No, not one!'

For a time, no one answered Harald's hoarse cries. Then a passing beggar-man, trundling a solid-wheeled cart, flung an armful of refuse – old rags, bones, and pieces of broken metal, into the cell.

This time Haro took a turn on his friend's shoulders and cried, 'The men of Miklagard are cowards! They are rats, ruled over by a puppy and a cat! Nothing more – just rats!'

The blind man in the corner cried out in fear at this, saying that the secret police of the city would surely hear and then they would all regret those words.

'For they will leave you no tongue with which to make your apologies,' he shouted.

But Haro shouted back, 'I am not the man to make apologies! I say that the men of this dunghill are cowards; such cowards as would be laughed to scorn along the fjords, where men take a pride in answering any challenge, whencesoever it comes!'

Suddenly, Haro noticed that the bustle outside the cell

window was still. A shadow fell upon his head and at eye level he saw a pair of feet, wearing heavy red and gilt sandals which reached so high that he lost them above the small window.

Once more he called out, 'I challenge any man, yes, any man, to combat; and I will bet my tongue that I will beat him in fair combat, though he has a sword and I a stick.'

And when Haro had finished, a deep voice from the street said loudly, 'Do you then, hairy one? Let us see what you have to say when I come down to you!'

The gilded feet passed from before the little opening, and then the sun shone down faintly into the cell again.

The old man clucked miserably to himself in the corner, while the two vikings stood back against the wall and waited for what should happen – each one already feeling the searing iron on his tongue, before his eyes, in imagination.

Then at last the grumbling gaoler flung open the door, and a man stood beside him on the upper steps – a man so immense that he had to bend to come under the doorway and down into the cell.

Harald stared at him in admiration, for he was a soldier and was dressed in all the golden glory of an officer of the Byzantine Guard. His purple cloak swung heavily behind him; his gilded scabbard slapped against his great thigh. This was a man above ordinary men, thought the vikings.

As he walked down among the rotting straw, he pinched his aquiline nose delicately and blew out his curled moustaches in disgust. Then he came on towards the two men, who stood to face him, trying to put on the bravest face that hunger and exhaustion would allow them.

'Which of you two challenged me a moment ago?' he said, his thin lips curled into a strange smile.

Both men spoke, 'I did!'

He smiled and then called to the old man who was praying in the corner, stiff with fear, 'Which of these two challenged me, old fellow?'

The old man said, 'I heard no one challenge anyone, lord.' The splendid soldier stood back for a moment, his hand on the hilt of his great sword.

Then he said lightly, 'Two heroes and a wise man in one small cell. I did not think Byzantium could boast such a gathering.'

His quick eyes surveyed the vikings from head to foot; it seemed to them that he noticed everything. And then, after a long silence, he said, 'To fight with you would be to waste good men, for I should assuredly kill you.'

The vikings burst out at this, suddenly angry, but he waved them to silence with a commanding gesture and went on, 'You are real men, I can see that; and warriors, I can see that also, from the scars you bear. I observe, moreover, that you come from the north – by your accent and by your fondness for bears' claw necklaces!'

Harald broke out, 'What is wrong with that? We killed the bears ourselves to get the necklaces! We did not buy our trinkets from any goldsmith's booth, my friend!'

For a moment the officer regarded Harald sternly, as he twisted his own gold chain between his strong brown fingers. But at last he smiled again and said, 'Have it your own way, northman. But let me speak; I say that I would not fight you and kill you – if such were my fortune; I would rather buy you and use your courage and your strength.'

Then for a moment his gaze rested on the old man in the corner. 'You are not of the north, I know, old one. You are one whom we all know, we of the Palace. Yet I will buy you too, and though I have no use for you, I think you could find a better home than this for yourself. What say you?'

But the old man shook his head. 'Thank you, Kristion,' he said. 'For it is Kristion, I know; no other man has such a voice and such a heavy footfall! No, thank you, Captain of the Guard, but I am too old and too weak to beg my bread in the streets where I once rode in glory.'

The Captain, Kristion, strode to him and took him by the shoulder. 'Don't be an old fool,' he said, smiling. 'You can go to my sister's house, in the country. Her children need a tutor. That would be easy for you, and the children are gentle little ones.'

He turned to the vikings. 'I offer you a place as soldiers in the Palace Guard – in Irene's Company. You will get food and clothes, and enough pay to enjoy yourselves on without being pampered. Will you come?'

Harald and Haro stepped forward, smiling, their hands held out. 'We will come,' they said. 'That is, if the old man will agree to leave this place too.'

And when the old man was turned round, so that the question could be put to him again, they saw that he was crying like a child.

The Captain, Kristion, turned away suddenly, flicking

his cloak hem over his own eyes. He went up the steps in silence, and at the top turned and said, 'There will be some trifling matter of signing the papers of purchase. I will return tomorrow, Guardsmen, have no fear. And when I do, see that you spring to attention. None of this northern slackness in my Company, my friends.'

Then the door was shut behind him, and the prisoners put their arms about each other, in glee, like children who had just been promised a wonderful present.

Harald lounged in the gateway of the great Palace, chuck-ling to himself in the sunshine. Everything was like a dream, he thought. Three weeks ago, he and Haro and the old man had been in prison, in the depths of despair. Now the old man was no doubt sunning himself and chattering in Greek or Latin to the children of Kristion's sister – and the vikings were full-blown guardsmen in the Palace of Irene !

Harald would hardly have believed it himself, if he had not his armour and weapons to prove it ! There was the fine bronze helmet, with the lion's head moulded on it, and the red horse's plume which swept half-way down his back; the purple cloak of thick Khazar wool, its hem weighted with small silver buttons shaped like acorns; the breastplate of polished silver with Irene's insignia em-blazoned on it in rich enamels of red and blue and deep yellow.

As for the weapons – Harald almost wept with pleasure at their rare beauty, and wished the folk along the fjord could have seen them – the long sword with the gold wire round its sharkskin hilt; the short broad dagger with the thin gold inlay along the blade; the javelin of ebony, butted with silver ... It was all like a dream, as was the great hall into which he looked from time to time.

Pillar after pillar rose like a forest of rich trees, and surmounted by semicircular arch after semicircular arch, until the mind grew confused with the intricacy of the design – and mosaic work everywhere, from floor to the high domed roof! Harald had long since stopped trying to find out who all the figures were in those delicate pictures; for even when he was told, by Kristion, who had taken the vikings round explaining everything to them before they were sworn in as guards, Harald had not understood what the names meant. Saints, Bishops, Emperors – they meant little to his mind, and so, in the torpor of the summer heat, he had decided to do the only possible thing, and ignore them, merely letting their magnificence shine down on him as he went about his duties.

Then, as he stood there in the bright light, his mind clouded with the memory that came back to him. A week before, he had first made the acquaintance of the great lady, Irene, mother of the Emperor-to-be, and the meeting had not been a pleasant one.

She had stormed into that very hall which lay behind him, a short elderly figure, her wrinkled face painted as brightly as that of a doll, her greying hair dyed an impossible shade of reddish-purple, her clumsy body made enormous by the billowing robes of thick brocade, heavily embroidered in gold and silver thread so that she rustled as she moved, like a forest with the wind blowing through it.

She had stopped before Harald and Haro and with her lips pinched tightly had said, in her coarse high voice, 'So these are the two northern fools who brought that Muslim baggage to Byzantium!'

Then, with a cruel sneer on her face, she had said, 'But
have no fears, northmen, you will never take her back
again! When I have finished with her, she will not be
worth taking anywhere!'

Kristion had been following the lady Irene in her inspection of the Guard and had winked at Harald when
the lady was talking to another man. Harald took some
comfort from that wink, for he felt that Kristion meant
to imply that Irene was merely threatening Marriba in
order to impress her own power upon the vikings.
Nevertheless, Harald had been worried, for Irene seemed
viciously selfish in all things. His anxiety for Marriba,
however, had soon been driven from his mind by what followed afterwards.

The golden trumpets had blown and then young Constantine had pranced into the great hall, followed by half
a Company of his Guards, the men who wore the black
plume in their helmets.

Defiantly he had paced to the centre of the hall, and
with his hand on his hip had surveyed his mother as she
walked the length of the line of her Guards.

At last she had turned and, surveying him with a
twisted smile, had said, 'There you are, little one! Your
nurses have been looking for you all day! You are really a
very bad boy, Constantine, to lead your mother such a
dance!' Turning to her Captain, Kristion, she had then
said, 'See that the little Emperor is tucked away safely,
Captain. If he runs wild with rough companions, there
is no knowing to what mischief he may get up!'

Against his will, Kristion had marched to the young
Prince and, bowing, had taken him by the arm.

Constantine's own Guards had parted to let the great Kristion escort his prisoner away, out of the hall. The young man's eyes had turned in anguish on his mother; his lips had tried to give the order to his own Guards to strike her down, there and then. But somehow, nothing had happened. Nothing, except that the boy had been put into a prison cell specially prepared for him, with all necessary comforts, next to his mother's own bedroom.

'And that,' said Kristion, mopping his broad brow as he told his own Company, 'is the end of Constantine, as far as ruling Byzantium is concerned. He stands no more chance of doing that, than I do of being elected King of the Franks! Not so much, perhaps!'

The Company of Irene's Guard had laughed loud at this, but in each man's heart there was a tiny shred of pity for the young man whose mother was willing to kill him, rather than let him thwart her ambitious claims to the throne of the Eastern Empire.

And so Harald thought of all this, as he stood in the sunshine, at the door of that great hall, that morning. What had happened to Marriba he did not know, and at the moment did not dare inquire, though he and Haro had told each other, whispering at night in their sleeping quarters, that, if the chance arose, they would give the girl what help they could, thoughtless as she had been, both to her father and to themselves.

Then, as Harald bent to pick up a pebble to throw at a white pigeon which was pecking away at the opal eyes of an alabaster statuette in the courtyard, he heard the sound of the golden trumpets once more, and stood to attention, expecting that some member of Irene's family might be entering from the city, through the high gates of black marble.

But another Guardsman, who stood at the corner of the hall, only laughed at him and told him not to stand to attention for a squad of his own Company.

'Where have they been?' asked Harald, quietly.

The other man called from behind his hand, 'Up north, comrade; they've been out a month now, escorting a party of merchants who went to do business with the Khazars, trading our silks, gold, and wine for their furs, honey, and wax. Oh yes, and their slaves – I forgot that! But perhaps it's tactless of me to mention it – since you yourself have only recently shaken off the yoke, as it were!'

Harald made a violent gesture to the man, pretending to be very angry with him, but the other Guard put his finger to his nose and said, 'Speak no ill of the Khazars in this Palace, friend, for the last Emperor, Leo, had a Khazar chieftain as his grandfather, so rumour has it!'

Harald would have asked more of this, for the name Khazar interested him; he knew that they were a great people who inhabited the vast plains far inland, and beyond the Black Sea, a warlike folk who often lived in great skin tents and travelled from place to place at grazing time with their herds, a race of warriors who swept down from time to time on outlying towns, riding their half-wild ponies like demons, to burn and pillage without fear of any man.

But there was no time to ask about all this, for the squad of Guards marched in smartly, despite their long desert journey, followed by the merchants who had come to pay their tribute to Irene – and then the slaves. There were perhaps a score of these, mainly bent and dispirited Tartar-folk, whose dull eyes proclaimed their defeat; but there was one among them who caught Harald's eye, for he was an old friend. He stood as tall as a man and half a man, and was as broad in the back as three men standing together. He held himself erect, and so towered over the small folk of the Steppeland.

Harald started from his post on the steps and called, 'Why, Grummoch, you old rogue! Why, Grummoch!'

The giant shambled forward, pushing the Guard aside carelessly, and ran to Harald, who threw down his javelin and embraced the gigantic fellow.

The squad halted and their Captain did not know what to do; the impatient merchants began to bleat that they had paid good money for this slave and were not going to have him spoiled like this.

But then Kristion appeared, his face stern, his hand on the hilt of his great sword.

'Sooner or later,' he said gravely, 'all the big mice get caught in our mousetrap, my friends. And this is a mouse we shall not let go again. You merchants have provided the great lady Irene with a new Guardsman. He will be the tribute you pay this time. Now you may go about your lawful business; I speak for Irene herself.'

The merchants began to cry out that they had paid an enormous sum for the giant, as much as they normally paid for three grown men, and were not going to let him go like that. Kristion turned on them such a face as made them quail.

'Very well,' he said, 'Irene will accept the rest of your merchandise in the place of this slave. Guard, see that the furs, honey, wax, and other things are delivered to the warehouses immediately.'

Only then did the merchants change their tune. And so Giant Grummoch came to Miklagard and, because of the great heart of Kristion, the Captain, became a Guard alongside his old friends, Harald and Haro – though it was a week before the smiths could beat out a breastplate and a sword to fit him!

Chapter 19 *A New Enemy*

Grummoch soon became a great favourite with the Guards, because of his immense strength and his good humour. Nor did he ever take advantage of his size when it came to combat practice – though he always asked for four helpings of anything at mealtimes, and was never refused! Indeed, Kristion sent an order to the cooks that they were to give the giant as many helpings as he asked for, as long as the other men did not go short.

Strangely enough, Irene hated him from the moment she first set eyes upon him, and he her. She had stood before him, taunting him, until Harald saw that the giant's temper was almost outworn. Luckily, Irene seemed to have noticed that too, for she moved away from him and vented the rest of her spite on some other unfortunate Guardsman.

Afterwards, Grummoch said humorously, 'Captain Kristion, keep a good watch over that old vixen, for one night when I feel reckless I may go to her room and gobble her up, crown and all!'

But Kristion had only smiled and passed down the line, without punishing the Guard for what, in another man, might have been construed as disloyalty.

Indeed, few of the men took Grummoch at all seriously. They did not even believe the tale he told of his travels over the last months, though Harald had no doubt that they were true, fantastic as they seemed.

After the shipwreck, Grummoch said, he had swum towards the shore, even though his legs were fastened with the iron gyves. Then, when his strength was fading and the sea was coming into his mouth, he had floated on to a half-submerged rock, where he had stayed that night, barely holding on with his failing muscles. The next morning he was found by a small fishing smack, and taken ashore to a little village still inhabited by Spaniards and not Moors. There he stayed for some days, getting back his strength and helping in whatever ways he could; and at last had started his great journey back towards the north, walking across country, through the mountains, and hoping to reach the land of the Franks.

In the mountains he had fallen in with a gang of robbers who had valued him for potentialities as a warrior, and he had helped them too, in certain ways which he would not divulge; but at last the Emperor of the Franks had sent a large party of soldiers to clear these ruffians out of the mountains and they had taken to the sea, hoping to return when the hue and cry had died down.

But unfortunately, they had been wrecked off Corsica and had lived in the woods like savages for some weeks before being captured by a pirate crew who sold them as slaves to some Bulgars.

After that, Grummoch's tale became very confused, for he had escaped many times and had been caught by this tribe and that, until at last, in a final bid for freedom, he had walked right into a camp of foraging Khazars, who had been delighted with their catch.

And so, many months after his capture, he was exchanged to the Byzantine merchants for forty rolls of silk and five amphora of red wine. And then he came to be a Guard in Irene's Company!

It was a great joy to Harald and Haro to see their giant again, for, to tell the truth of it, they had already begun to feel somewhat lonely, out of place, and cut off, in this swarming palace of olive-skinned men and women – courtiers, officials, soldiers, hangers-on round the immensely powerful Irene.

One evening, when the stars speckled the dark blue sky and the three Guardsmen sat about a small brazier on one of the upper ramparts of the palace, Haro said, 'This is no place for us, my brothers. Here men speak one thing and think another. You cannot trust their eyes, they are dark-brown and sly; they always slide away from one's gaze.'

Grummoch nodded and said in his slow way, 'Yes, and always they seem to smile when they speak, as though they are already making some new plot to deceive one.'

Harald was sitting thoughtfully a little away from them. He rose and came over to the brazier slowly.

'I have been thinking,' he said, 'that now we are together, we should try to do something for Marriba. She was a foolish girl, I know, but then most girls are foolish, I have been led to understand, so she is no rarity. From the rumours which come into this place daily, I understand that Constantine will never be allowed to marry her. Indeed, a water-seller in the street yesterday called out, in my hearing, to a friend of his on the other side of the road, that Irene had sworn to put the girl to the torture.'

Haro started and said, 'How could he know that, a simple water-seller?'

'I took him by the arm,' said Harald, 'and held my sword point ever so slightly inclined towards his heart, as I asked him the same question. He was ready enough to answer me, and said that he had it from one of the cooks who usually took the water from him. She had it from a serving-wench who was in Irene's room at a private feast she gave to some of the counsellors. Irene had been drinking much wine, when suddenly she flung down her crystal goblet, breaking it to a thousand shivers in her anger. Then it was that she had burst out with the threat. Her son, she said, had been tempted to rebel against his mother's gentle guidance by this young Moslem hussy, and the sooner the girl was shown that it was dangerous to anger the Most High, the better.'

Grummoch said in his slow voice, 'Do you know where Marriba may be found, Harald?'

Harald nodded. 'Come over here,' he said. 'Now look where I am pointing. Can you see where the avenue of cypresses meets that tall white building with the pointed tower, away beyond the market square? Marriba lives on the second floor of a house near there, a house with a silver star painted above its archway. The water-seller showed me where it was, for I threatened him with torments for spreading palace rumours.'

Suddenly Haro straightened himself and stood up. 'Could you find your way there in the darkness, Harald?' he said.

Harald nodded his head slowly, 'I could do that, my friend,' he said. 'The same thought had come to me as I sat thinking, but I was not sure then whether you two would be prepared to help the girl.'

Grummoch smiled and answered, 'I would prefer that she were the daughter of the High King of Erin, for she is, or was, my own betrothed; but in cases like this, a man does not inquire about a girl's family or attachments before he gives her the help she needs. I am with you, Harald, come what may.'

'And I,' said Haro simply. 'You did not need to ask.'

Harald drew his friends close to him and whispered, 'Good, then, my brothers. We will start as soon as the Guard at the main gate begins his tour of the outer wall. Then we shall reach the street without anyone knowing.'

Giant Grummoch rubbed his great hands with glee. 'I have spent so much time evading capture of one sort and another, such things as this are second nature to me now, friend viking! But, one thing troubles me, what shall we do when we find her? We cannot bring her back here.'

'No,' said Haro, 'nor dare we try to take her away from Miklagard, for if we were caught, we should pay the worst sort of penalty as deserters from the Imperial Guard.'

Harald nodded and said, 'I have already thought of that. We shall merely remove her to another place, until such time as we can get her safely away from this city of corruption and intrigue. I had thought that we might get her away to Kristion's sister in the country, but that would place the Captain in an awkward position, since Irene trusts him entirely. So it will be best to put the girl in some little house in a back street, the house of such a man as my water-seller, for example, where she would never be suspected of hiding.'

Haro said, with a strange smile, 'There is one great problem – suppose she refuses to believe us that she is in danger? Suppose she refuses to come with us?'

Grummoch flexed his great arms and said, 'In my time, I have carried two grown calves at once. Surely I can manage a young girl!'

Harald grinned and answered, 'I do not know, giant. A young girl of this sort might well turn out to be difficult, even for such a man as you.'

Just then Haro pointed down over the courtyard; the guard was presenting his javelin and coming up to attention, as they did when they were about to set off on a tour of the outer wall.

'Come,' said Harald, 'now is our chance!'

Removing their bright helmets so that the starlight should not give them away, glistening on the burnished metal, they bent their heads and moved along the wall and so down the first staircase that led to the courtyard.

But before they reached the lower stairway, Harald held up his hand for them to stop. They did so and followed his gaze; he was staring at a small round window in the inner wall of the stair-well. The flicker of candle-light came through the aperture and also the sound of voices – two voices, a woman's and a boy's, the first insistent and domineering, the other high and tremulous, the voice of a coward, or one almost out of his wits with terror.

Harald crept to the window, holding his scabbard

tightly lest it should rattle against the wall and give them away. He looked down into a room almost as high and narrow as a water-well. From the many chains and gyves which hung from the walls, he knew what this place was – the torture chamber. But it was not the irons and manacles which caught the viking's eye – it was the two people in that horrible room – Irene and her weak son, Constantine. The boy lay grovelling among the straw on the stone floor, his legs chained to the wall, his arms stretched out in supplication.

'I will promise to do anything you say, Mother of Glory,' he moaned, 'only do not leave me in this cell another night. I am frightened by the sounds that come in through the window when all the Palace is asleep. They seem to gibber and grunt at me, mocking me . . .'

Irene smiled bitterly and pushed the boy's head back with her sandalled foot.

'I should think they *do* gibber and grunt at you, you fool! That is all the sense you seem to understand, gibberings and grunts!' she said. She paused for a while then and half-turned away from the weeping Prince. Then so softly that Harald had difficulty in hearing her words, she said, 'There are ways of preventing such things from troubling you, brave one. There are ways of stopping unpleasant sounds from reaching one's ears . . . just as there are ways of stopping a man from seeing things which disturb him. You understand me, O Emperor?'

As she spoke, Constantine began to howl with terror, trying again and again to grasp the fringe at the edge of her robe.

'Great Mother, Dear One, Sweetest One,' he cried, 'do

not hurt me, I beg you! I will do anything, anything, if you will not let them hurt me!'

Irene looked down on her son in immense contempt, her cruel eyes narrowed, her cruel lips smiling wickedly. 'So,' she said in her deep voice, 'this is the little puppet that thought itself an Emperor of the Roman World! This is the man who would lead an army to glory, is it?'

Harald bit his lip and whispered savagely, 'If I had a little bird bow here now I could rid Byzantium of a devil, a she-devil!

Haro shook his head sadly, 'Constantine is not worth it, my friend,' he said. 'He is as cruel as his mother and would give you no thanks. Consider, had it not been for good Kristion, we should still be rotting in prison because of this coward, Constantine.'

They stopped whispering then, because Irene's voice had begun once more.

'Very well, my little one,' she said, 'perhaps I will forget your wickedness to me this once. Soon I will send the paper to you to sign. You shall declare that you have named me to act as your Regent, and a number of other small things ... Including your solemn oath not to marry this Moslem wench. Now that I come to consider it, you shall also sign that she is to be put to death, without delay, for inciting you to break the settled peace of your great City. I will have that drawn up tomorrow. Do you promise to sign it?'

Constantine flung himself face downwards in a spasm of relief. 'Yes, dear mother,' he almost shouted, 'I will sign it a thousand times, if you will set me free.'

Irene gazed upon him again and said, 'There, you are

overwrought, little one. Perhaps you are a good boy, after
all! Wait patiently until tomorrow when I can get the
scribe to make out such a paper, and then, when you have
put your mark on it, you shall go free. Or at least, almost
free, for I cannot have you wandering outside the Palace,
getting into trouble again.'

Harald turned from the window suddenly. 'Come on,'
he said, 'it seems that we must act tonight, before that
paper may become the law.'

They ran down the lower staircase, and across the
courtyard. From the Officers' Mess, they saw the amber
light streaming, and heard the sound of merry voices singing a camp song; Kristion's voice was loud and clear,
ringing high above all other voices. The three soldiers ran
on and passed through the gateway and into the darkness, just as the sentry finished his circuit of the wall and
came once more into view.

As they went, keeping to the lonelier streets, Harald
said, 'So Constantine is a new enemy! The coward, so to
sign away the life of one who loves him, however silly
she may be in giving her heart to such a little monster!'

Haro said grimly, 'Perhaps we can get even with him,
before our stay in this den of wild beasts is finished.'

Then they came to the place where the avenue of cypresses met the white tower, and Harald suddenly stopped
and drew his companions back into the shadow of a column. His eyes were wide open in surprise and bewilderment. 'Look,' he said hoarsely 'we are forestalled!'

The others followed the pointing finger and saw the
glitter of breastplates and shields in the light which
strayed from the many windows of the square.

All along the narrow street, and across the archway which led to Marriba's lodging, soldiers were posted, men of Irene's own Company, there was no mistaking their helmet plumes and breastplate insignia . . .

Haro struck himself hard upon the chest, as though angry with the part he had played. 'If only we had got here more quickly . . .' he groaned.

But Harald shook his head, 'Irene is making sure,' he whispered. 'She is not one to take chances, my friend. I have no doubt that these men have been stationed here all day long. We must not reproach ourselves. Now there is nothing we can do, except go back to the Palace. Perhaps tomorrow, we may think of something.'

Haro said sharply, 'It will be a bad thing for Marriba if we do not act more quickly than we have done tonight.'

They turned then and walked quickly back along the street, keeping in the shadow of the high houses. Grummoch followed his comrades like an immense shadow, keeping watch that they were not attacked from behind.

The day which followed passed on leaden wings. The two vikings and giant Grummoch were unable to settle down to do anything as it should be done. First they were reprimanded for not making up their beds in the official manner; then they were reported by the head cook for not sweeping out the hall properly, after the morning meal; and before midday, they were threatened with twenty lashes for not burnishing their breastplates so that a man's face could be seen in them clearly, as was the custom among the Imperial Guard.

The sergeant who threatened them glared fiercely down as they sat cross-legged in the shadow of a bath-house.

'You northmen,' he stormed, 'are fit for nothing but shovelling cattle fodder! Why I have to train such fools as you, I cannot tell; I must have committed some great sin in a former life and this is my punishment.'

Giant Grummoch lazily took up a javelin and, holding it in his two hands, suddenly snapped the ash-shaft with a quick movement. Then, just as lazily, he said in his shrill voice, 'I am sorry the little spear broke, sergeant. I am used to stronger weapons.'

Then he rose to his feet, as heavily as a laden ox, and turned towards the sergeant, his great hands outstretched. The man backed from him, his dark eyes starting in sudden fear.

But Grummoch only smiled, the corners of his broad mouth turning up slightly, and said, 'If you will give me another spear, sergeant, I will see that it does not happen again.'

The sergeant mopped his brow with relief, and trying to regain some of his former composure, said, 'Very well, Guardsman, you shall have another spear. But do not let that accident happen to the new one. You may dismiss!'

Grummoch sat down again, smiling, and pretending to fit the two broken pieces together again.

Haro grinned and said, 'I have not seen a man so frightened for a long time.'

Harald said, 'You saw one last night, when his mother was threatening him with torture.'

But Haro shook his head. 'No,' he said, 'that was not a man – just a small and treacherous beast.'

It was at this moment that a Guard staggered in from the town where he had been on patrol in the big open market, keeping order among the swarming traders. His face was white and fearful. They saw the sweat glistening on his forehead, beneath the peak of his bronze helmet.

'Have you any water, comrades?' he said, suddenly slumping down beside them on the stone pavement. Grummoch flung his water-bottle to the man, who drank greedily.

'What is the matter, friend?' asked Harald.

The man turned towards him, his mouth quivering. 'Something is wrong,' he said. 'It is as though the scent of death hangs over the city today. Three times I have seen a man stop in the midst of his bargaining and fall to the ground, with the white froth on his lips. It is not good, my friend.'

As he spoke, the bright sky seemed suddenly to cloud, with a heavy sulphurous lowering. The man wiped the sweat from his face and got up slowly.

'It seems that you have a fever, comrade,' said Grummoch. 'You should report to your Captain.'

The man nodded and staggered away, dragging his long javelin on the stones behind him.

When he had gone, Harald said, 'I do not like the look of that. No Guard I have ever seen trailed his javelin in that manner.'

Grummoch said quietly, 'I do not think that we shall ever go on parade with that one again, my friend. He had a strange look about the eyes which I have seen before – but never twice in the eyes of the same man.'

They were about to speak more on this matter when the high snarling trumpet called out that they were to assemble for a surprise inspection in the great courtyard. Instantly men came running from all directions, buckling on their equipment as they ran. The three friends rose and joined their ranks.

Then Irene appeared, strolling slowly through the high arched doorway of the Palace, her painted face set in a grim smile. The Guardsmen stood as straight and as motionless as though they had been carved from stone, though in the intense heat the strain was immense.

Irene moved between the ranks with a painful slowness, as though she meant to test the endurance of her soldiers to the utmost. One young lad in the rear rank suddenly gave a groan and fell face downwards, his shield and spear clattering onto the paved courtyard beside him. His comrades on either side instantly leapt forward to raise him, but Irene's voice cut harshly through the heavy air.

'Let the dog lie,' she said. 'He must suffer for his weakness. My Guards must be men of iron or must die in their weakness.'

She paused a moment and then said to Kristion, 'Have those two who broke the ranks whipped before the sun goes down. Fifty lashes apiece. That should teach them to stand like soldiers when their Empress does them the honour of visiting them.'

Kristion frowned, but could do nothing at that moment. He nodded to a sergeant who marched the two Guardsmen away to the barrack-block.

Then Irene was level with the three friends and they saw that she held a small roll of paper in her right hand, decorated with the Imperial seal. They had no doubt that this was the document which Constantine had signed, the death-warrant of Marriba.

Irene paused a little while in front of them, smiling as she surveyed them from head to toe. Grummoch felt his legs suddenly quivering, as though the muscles would stand this strain no longer than might make him run forward and strike this woman down.

But she passed on then, and at last returned to the Palace.

When she had gone, Kristion returned to his Company and said, 'Guardsmen, you may dismiss; but hold yourselves in readiness should the Most High require your services before this day is out.'

As the three friends were moving away, he called

them and said, 'You heard what the Most High said, about giving those Guardsmen fifty lashes apiece? Well, go and whip them.'

Harald said, 'Do you mean that, Captain?'

Kristion turned a strangely humorous gaze upon the viking and said, 'I have given my order; but I did not say what you were to whip them with. Use your discretion, Guardsman.'

So it was that the three northmen surprised the prisoners greatly by tying them up gently and whipping them with a length of helmet ribbon, such as was worn on festive occasions, a thin silk braid. After which, they reported back to Kristion that the prisoners had been well whipped, with a few extra strokes for good measure.

He smiled and said, 'Good; now release them. They are two of my best soldiers – and no doubt, two of your best friends from this day on.'

And so it turned out to be.

Later that afternoon, a provisioner they all knew and trusted – an unusual situation as far as the city traders were concerned – trundled his empty fruit barrow into the courtyard, and spreading his hands in despair bewailed the loss of his goods.

'My lords,' he wailed, 'my business is ruined! All my lovely fruits have been stolen! I was stopped in the street and robbed, I tell you!'

A sergeant who was passing took the man by his arm and shook him, pretending to be angry.

'You rogue,' he said, 'you know well enough that you have sold the fruit intended for us at twice the price to some unsuspecting trader from Khazaria!'

The provisioner shook his head violently and almost wept.

'No, lord, no !' he said vehemently. 'A crowd of ruffians knocked me down – look, here is the bruise – and took my fruit ! They said that now the plague has come to the city, it is every man's right to take what he can, while there is anything to take.'

At these words, the chattering groups of soldiers fell silent. The sergeant's smile faded from his sunburnt face.

'Are you sure that the plague has truly come, old friend?' he asked.

The tradesman beat his thin breast in anguish.

'Sure !' he echoed, 'Sure? I should think I am sure ! Has not my own brother's mother-in-law passed away with it this very day? Is not my third cousin's youngest child sickening with it this very minute?'

The sergeant flung the man a handful of coins and turned to the assembled soldiers.

'Make ready,' he said abruptly. 'You may be needed in the city at any time now, for riots will break out and shops be broken into when the news spreads.'

Then he marched off to inform the Chamberlain of the grave occasion.

The late afternoon sun had sunk and the first twilight was creeping over the white city, when Kristion strode into the courtyard. His face was set and his eyes narrow. He walked among the men, who stood waiting for any order which he might give, and carefully chose five Guardsmen, telling them to stand to one side. They were the three friends and the two who had been whipped with helmet ribbons that morning. The other Guardsmen stood staring at them, wondering what duty had so suddenly been assigned to them. At that moment, no one envied them, for suddenly the city had become a place of danger, of ill-omen, almost of terror.

Then Kristion stood the five men to attention and addressed them, saying, 'Men, you have been chosen to perform a task of some unpleasantness, but one which you must not shirk if you are loyal to the Most High, Irene, and to your Company. You will march as a squad to a house in the city, led by myself, and there you will do what you are commanded.'

Harald looked him in the eye. 'Captain,' he said quietly, so that only his immediate companions heard his words, 'is the unpleasant duty to do with a certain lady from Jebel Tarik?'

For a moment, Kristion stared back at Harald as though he did not know whether to punish him or not. But at last he nodded slowly.

'I have the Imperial warrant here,' he said, touching the roll of paper with the seal, which they had last seen in Irene's hand that morning.

Then, before the three could frame another question, or even think of what they should do, Kristion formed them up and led them out of the main gate.

The sentry sprang smartly to attention as they passed and raised his javelin, crying, 'May good fortune ever smile on Her!'

Kristion nodded curtly and said, as he returned the salute, 'May She prosper!'

But Harald, who marched nearest to the Captain,

noticed that as he spoke those words, his thin lips curled in bitterness.

As the squad marched on through the darkening streets, Harald stole a glance at Haro, who stared back and suddenly made a gesture of running his forefinger across his throat and nodding towards Kristion, who was gazing ahead. But Harald shook his head; Kristion had already been too good a friend to them.

At the end of the first narrow street, they came out into a small square, surrounded by high white buildings and edged with dark trees. At the base of each tree, and huddled in every archway, figures lay wrapped in robes, shrouds, lengths of sacking, anything that could be put to that final and dreadful purpose. In the middle of the square, a great brazier smouldered, throwing off the thick smoke of sulphur and casting a low-lying cloud of yellow vapour, which hung head-high across that forlorn place.

Kristion halted his squad and half-turned to them.

'The plague has struck heavily here,' he began. Then he gave a short gasp and put his hand to his forehead suddenly, knocking off his light ceremonial helmet. The Guardsmen gazed at him in bewilderment and saw the beads of sweat break out on his olive skin, the light froth which gathered at his lips of a sudden, flecking his dark beard. As they watched him, he swung round as though trying to avoid a blow, then staggered away from them and fell, breathing harshly, against the wall.

Harald ran towards him, 'Captain,' he said, 'what ails you?'

Kristion looked at him as though he were a stranger,

or as though he could hardly see. Then he shook his head and tried to smile.

'Viking,' he gasped, 'it is the wish of the Most High, Irene, that I strike off the head of the girl, Marriba, to-night. She commanded me to take a squad and see that this was done ... That is why I chose you and your friends, and those two who owe you something and will obey you ...'

The Captain's voice failed him for a moment, as Harald said, 'But Kristion, I could never have helped you to do such a thing, you know that.'

The Captain of the Imperial Guard slid down the wall until he rested on his knees on the pavement. He looked up at Harald and smiled.

'I know that well enough, my friend. That is why you are here with me now,' he said weakly.

Then slowly and with fumbling fingers, he untied the purple sash which was his Captain's emblem, and held it out towards Harald.

'Viking,' he said, 'I am a sick man, I know that; I have seen too many smitten with this plague not to know the signs of death. Take this sash and put it on. Then go forward and do as you think is right in this matter.'

Harald took the sash, wondering at the Captain's courage, and slowly wrapped it about his waist.

Kristion, the great Captain, watched him with a still smile, then, raising his right hand in salute he croaked, 'Hail, Captain of the Guard in Byzantium!'

As he finished his greeting, he fell forward onto the stones of the pavement and lay still. Haro ran to pick him up, but Harald waved him away and said, 'There is nothing that we can do, my brother. It is the will of whatever God he prayed to. Let us go quickly and take advantage of this change in our fortune.'

As the others moved away, Harald stooped and patted the Captain Kristion on the shoulder, as though he were alive again and knew what was happening.

Then he hastened on after the four Guards.

As they marched on along the tree-lined avenue, Haro said, 'That was a good man and a true soldier we have left lying in the street, comrades.'

Harald said, 'If all Christians were like that one, there is not a true man who would not be a Christian. Kristion is just such another man as the priest, John, who once held me up in the sea until the Danish longship rescued me. I have often thought about that. I owe my life to a Christian, and soon, perhaps, another will owe her life to one. When I get the opportunity, friend Haro, I shall burn ten candles in a Christian church for Kristion, if his God will accept the offering.'

Haro replied, 'I think that He will, Harald; He seems an understanding God to me, after what I know of Thor and Odin.'

As they talked in this manner, they passed many folk lying in doorways, inert or groaning; and here and there, at the street corners, they glimpsed small groups of men with angry faces, who melted into the dusk as the soldiers came up to them. Over all the city there was the heavy stench of sulphur and of green herbs, which had been flung on to the many braziers and street fires to keep away the plague.

So at last they came to the white tower where Marriba had her lodging. Four Guardsmen stood before the archway which led into her house, looking impatiently to left and to right, as though they were tired of their long vigil.

When Harald marched up to them, they sprang to attention, seeing his Captain's sash.

'Greetings, Captain,' said their sergeant, who stared at the viking in surprise when he recognized him. 'These are good times for quick promotion.'

Harald sensed the old soldier's resentment and replied, 'That is a question for you to discuss with the Most High. She will no doubt be interested to hear your remarks on her choice of Officers.'

The sergeant dropped his eyes and mumbled, 'I meant no offence, Captain.'

Harald stared at him impassively. 'Very well, sergeant,' he said. 'March your men away immediately and report to the Palace. We have come to relieve you.'

Without another word, the sergeant saluted and then turned and called his men together. As they marched away across the square, Grummoch said, 'It was good to me to see the look on that sergeant's face!'

Harald smiled bitterly and said, 'It is the first order I have given, as Captain of the Guard in Byzantium; it may well be my last!'

Then quietly he whispered to Haro to follow him into the house, and told the others to wait outside for him, keeping well in the shadow of the building.

'Do not let anyone come up these stairs,' he told them. 'No, not the Most High herself!'

The soldiers nodded, for already they had come to like this quiet viking who assumed power so easily without assuming the arrogance which too often goes with it.

On the first landing of the stairway, Harald said, 'Stay here, friend Haro. Come up only if I call you. Do not let anyone follow after me, for what I go to do must be kept a secret.'

Haro said, 'I would hold back the whole of Irene's Company.'

Harald smiled down at him in friendship, then drawing his short sword he flung open the door and entered.

The old woman, Lalla, gave a cry of terror and dragged her skirts over her head, shrinking back among the cushions on the floor. Marriba sat on a small gilded stool in the middle of the room. She did not move as Harald strode across the floor towards her, but smiled quietly, looking past him into space.

'Strike quickly, soldier,' she said, as though she was inviting him to sit down, or to taste some sweetmeat that lay on the little table beside her. 'Strike quickly and cleanly,' she repeated. 'I have been expecting you for three days and I do not wish to wait any longer.'

Harald fell on his knees before her, amazed at her courage, and laid his sword in her lap. Only then did her gaze come back within the four walls of the room, and she looked down at him with a gentle surprise, recognizing him in spite of the great peak of his bronze helmet.

She put her hand on his shoulder for an instant and said, 'Why, have you been given this unpleasant task, then? How cruel of Irene to make you do it.'

But Harald shook his head and said urgently, 'I have come to give you your freedom in another way, Marriba. Come, there is no time to waste, you must do as I say.'

She paused for a moment and said shyly, 'Constantine

... has he sent no message? Has he not tricked his mother and sent me a message?'

Harald turned his face away, unwilling to look the girl in the eyes when he told her the savage truth of the matter, yet knowing that the truth must be told.

'Lady,' he said as gently as he could, 'Constantine was unfaithful to you; he even signed your death warrant so that he might not be put to any further inconvenience. He is unworthy of you, Marriba; you must forget him and take your chance of freedom.'

She stood up then and said simply, 'Yes, I think I knew it, but I hoped against hope that he might have found strength from somewhere. Very well, viking, what am I to do?'

Harald took back the sword which she offered him and said, 'First, I would be pleased if you would scream; something rather sharp and frightening, lady; for, after all, I am supposed to be here for a sharp and frightening business!'

Marriba smiled sadly, then she went to the window and screamed. Harald was quite taken aback by the convincing sound which the girl produced. He heard the voices of the soldiers in the street stop suddenly, as though they too had been taken in. Then Harald went to the door and opened it. Haro was standing outside, his own sword out, his eyes wild.

'It is all right, my friend,' said Harald smiling. 'No harm has come to her; you may go back to your post.'

Then, though much against her will, the sword which had been brought to that house for one purpose was used for another; swiftly, Harald cut off the girl's long hair, looking away as each thick tress fell to the floor. Then, with the help of Lalla, who had by now come round, he knotted a small turban on Marriba's head and tucked her long gown about her so that it looked like a tunic.

Afterwards he stood back and said, 'You make a very pleasant-looking boy. You must take care that some silly young girl does not fall in love with you before you reach your father's house at Jebel Tarik once again.'

Marriba suddenly fell upon her knees before Harald, clasping his hands tightly. 'My dear friend,' she said. 'I do not deserve such a protector as you. And am I really going back to my father?'

Harald said grimly, 'If you do not reach your father's house safe, it will be because Haro lies dead on the ground. He will take you back, lady.'

Marriba said slowly, 'But it is so far and we have no money.'

Harald answered quietly, 'Haro has found his way half across the world on more than one occasion; travelling is nothing new to him. He has a sword and a ready tongue; I have no doubt that, before morning, he will have found money, one way or another – though it strikes me that he is more likely to find a boat for the two of you. That is more in his line and would be much more useful than money.'

Harald went to the door and called Haro within. Quickly he told him what they had planned, and as he spoke, Haro nodded solemnly, as though he had expected it all along.

Then Harald turned to go. 'Stay here, my friends,' he said, 'until I have taken my men out of sight of this house.

Then make your way down to the harbour by the back streets. One day we may all meet again. Farewell!'

Suddenly Haro clasped him by the hands, and Marriba flung her arms about him.

'We cannot let you go,' said the girl, in tears. 'Come with us, Harald, and I will see that my father makes you a rich man!'

Harald turned his back on them, for he suddenly found that his eyes were becoming damp too. He shook his head.

'No,' he said, 'I have no wish to live out my days in Spain, thank you. Besides, friend Grummoch would feel lonely. Also, I have a hankering to see something more of the world before I settle down. No, I must go my way. Take care of her, Haro; and good-bye, lady.'

As he went back into the street, he was careful to be seen wiping the blade of his sword. But Grummoch was not deceived. A roguish smile played about his thick lips, but he said nothing.

One of the other soldiers said, 'Where is Haro, Captain?'

Harald nodded back up the stairs. 'I have left him to guard the body,' he said. 'The Most High would wish that; she might want to make one of her inspections, you know.'

The two men stared at Harald, a strange light playing in their eyes. 'It is well that we are all in this affair together,' said one of them.

Harald asked, 'What do you mean by that, Guardsman?'

The soldier began to shoulder his long javelin. 'I mean that we are men who can keep a secret, Captain,' he replied. His companion nodded in agreement, smiling. Then they began to march back to the Palace.

When they reached the spot where Kristion had fallen with the plague, Harald stopped and spread his own cloak over the body, and put the purple sash over the Captain's chest.

Then he stepped back and gave Kristion a final salute.

'We shall not see such a man again, my friends,' he said. They did not reply, but looked down on the still Captain with gentle eyes. Then they marched on towards the high Palace walls. Once inside, Harald told the men to wait while he reported that the duty had been carried out successfully.

As he strode across the coloured tiles of the great hall, he almost ran into the Chamberlain, who was bustling out, breathless, his face wet with sweat, his hands shaking with anxiety. Harald saluted him, raising his flat hand out above his head, after the custom of the Imperial Guard.

'Hail, my lord,' he said. 'I bring a message for the Most High.'

The Chamberlain stopped and stared at him as though he were some unusual wild creature brought from foreign parts.

'The Most High?' he said. 'The Most High? Why, Irene is not here. No, she left for Chrysopolis, across the water, half an hour ago. She and the Prince – they think the air will be cleaner there – less danger of plague. And I must be going too, my dear fellow. Really, I must. The boat is waiting for me, down at the quay. You must excuse me.'

He began to totter past Harald, who called after him, 'When you see the Most High, my lord, tell her that we carried out our duty. Marriba will never trouble her again.'

The Chamberlain did not even stop or turn round, but shambled on, nodding, his face streaked with fear. 'Yes, my dear fellow,' he muttered. 'I won't forget ... No, I won't forget.'

Harald smiled grimly after him, then he too turned and went to where his men stood waiting for him, realizing that now there was no one in authority to whom he could report the death of Kristion.

Chapter 22 *City in Flames*

As Harald made his way towards the small postern where he had left his friends, his mind was clouded with doubts. Obviously the Palace would soon be left to the care of what remained of the Imperial Guard, since both Irene and her ministers were fleeing from the plague and would undoubtedly be away from Byzantium as long as there was any danger of the disease spreading. Moreover, it was likely that within a few days at the most, death would be so rampant within the city that the Guard would become virtually imprisoned within the Palace walls, for fear of infection.

And that might become inconvenient for at least two reasons; food supplies would be scarce, and the Palace would become the unfailing target for any unrest which arose among the suffering population of the city's poorer districts.

As Harald turned over these thoughts in his mind, an angry red glow was flung across the sky from the northern suburbs of Byzantium. Hardly had this appeared, when a smaller flush spread over the low clouds to the west.

Harald turned in time to see a third area of sky glowing a dull bronze-red. There could be no mistaking such signs. The rebellious elements of the city, having heard, no doubt, that their rulers had deserted them, were taking the law into their own hands, and were setting fire to those parts of the city which were unprotected.

Grummoch met Harald and said, 'This is what I expected, friend. Do we stay and roast, or do we set out on our travels again, to see what else the world holds for a pair of likely fellows?'

Harald turned to catch the eyes of the two soldiers who had moved up close behind him and were waiting for his answer.

'What say you, my friends?' Harald asked them. 'Will you stay in the Palace and risk starving, or will you come for a little walk with us, to see what the world is like outside Miklagard?'

The elder of the soldiers took Harald by the hand. 'Friend,' he said, 'nothing would please us better than to go walking with you; but my friend Justinian and I have wives and children over the water at Pera. It runs in our minds to go now and comfort them.'

Harald said, 'You are wise men, my friends. Go, and one day I hope we may meet again.'

The two men threw their swords and javelins into a corner and ran swiftly towards the great open gate. Harald heard them joking with the Guard who lolled there, telling him that they were only going as far as the next corner, by the sergeant's orders, to see if the night breeze was fanning the fires. Then they disappeared.

'We might try the same trick,' said Grummoch. 'But it would be wise for us to walk in the opposite direction.'

Harald nodded and they walked towards the gate, without their javelins but hiding their swords beneath their tunics.

'Halt!' shouted the Guard, suspiciously. 'Where do you walk, men?'

Grummoch answered, 'We go at the sergeant's orders to see if the fires are being fanned by the night's breeze, Guardsman.'

The man smiled cynically and shook his head. 'You know the rules as well as I do, my little man,' he said. 'Only two allowed out at one time, except by special pass. Have you a pass?'

It was in Grummoch's mind to march up to the man and show him his great ham of a fist and to tell him that this was his pass. But at that moment there sounded a sudden scurry of many feet down the narrow street and a mob of excited townsfolk came into view, yelling and waving sticks and rough weapons.

'Down with Irene, the she-wolf!' they shouted. 'Down with her idiot of a son! They have brought disaster upon us! The Bishops warned us that we risked damnation in supporting Irene! The Bishops are right! Where is Irene? We will slay her and her son! We will burn her Palace of Unrighteousness! Down with Irene! Down with the Guard! They are butchers! They are the hounds of their evil Mistress!'

The Guard at the gate calmly lowered his javelin, which had prevented the passage of Harald and Grummoch. Then he drew a silver whistle from his belt-pouch and blew a shrill blast upon it.

'You two had better go and get your javelins, my friends,' he said with a cold smile to Harald and Grummoch.

Behind them, in the barrack block, a trumpet began to

sound the 'Fall in !' The two men heard the sound of their comrades' feet pattering on the stone courtyard.

They were caught between the mob and the Imperial Guard.

Just then stones began to fly. One struck Grummoch on the chest, but did him no harm; another struck the sentry between the eyes. He fell like a slain ox and lay still.

Grummoch rolled him aside and said, 'Come on, Harald, or we shall be too late !'

Then, with a great roar, he drew his sword from under his tunic and charged at the crowd. Harald came beside him, shouting out with all his strength, 'Up the North ! Death to all traitors !'

The mob faded before them, like wisps of smoke before a fierce gust of wind. Suddenly the street was empty and then Grummoch said, 'Come on, lad, or we'll be caught again !'

They turned and ran with all their speed away from the Palace gate, and did not stop for breath until they were once more in the centre of the city.

They stood panting beside a tamarisk-tree when Harald said suddenly, 'I have seen the light, friend Grummoch ! Look, do you notice a house at the end of that alley-way, with a door shaped like a Frankish shield set on its end? Well, that house was once described to me by an old man, when I was in prison here. It is one of the secret treasure houses of Her Imperial Majesty – one of many, scattered about the city.'

Grummoch ruminated like a great bull. 'I recall what a splendid store of treasure I once had, little Harald, way back in the kingdom of MacMiorog of Dun-an-oir. That treasure I lost – you know how ! I would like to reimburse myself for it, somehow, before I die.'

Harald nodded and said, 'Irene owes us a month's pay, Grummoch; and we served her well. After all, did we not dispose of Marriba for her? Come on, let us see what is to be found there !'

The door shaped like a shield opened easily when they set their shoulders to it, and they found themselves faced by a narrow stone passage-way, at the far end of which was a small square courtyard, set round on three sides with squat pillars.

Harald ran straightway to a square flagstone in the middle of the courtyard. There was an iron ring set into it.

'This is the place,' he said excitedly. 'The old man described it all – even the iron ring. If we lift that flagstone, we shall find a flight of steps leading directly into the cellar where the gold is stowed.'

Grummoch had taken the ring firmly in his hand when a light shone on them from behind. As they turned in surprise, a man came from behind one of the squat pillars, a long curved sword in his right hand.

'You choose the right moment, my lords,' he said in a sly and silky voice. 'But, alas, you forget that I am the official guardian of what lies below.'

Harald stared him in the eye and said, 'We are Guardsmen of the Company of the Most High. We come at her command, to bring back treasure for her, to pay for anything she might require while she is away from Byzantium.'

The man gazed at Harald for a long while and then

began to smile. 'Indeed,' he said. 'Yet only an hour ago a messenger came from the Most High, threatening me with a slow death if as much as a single plate were moved from its place when she got back from Chrysopolis! How do you account for that, then, my good fellows?'

Grummoch shrugged his massive shoulders and walked a pace towards the man, until the point of the curved sword was almost touching his throat. He folded his arms so that the guardian of the treasure should not feel suspicious and then, with a queer little smile on his lips, said, 'Once in Erin, in the kingdom of the High King of Drumnacoigh, there was a treasure house, much bigger than this. And the guardian of that house was a warrior, such as you might be yourself, but with an unusual equipment for the job; he had an eye set in the back of his head, just below where the hair grows thickest.'

The Byzantine guard smiled with malice and said, 'I have heard such stories before, my friend. Do not come any nearer.'

Grummoch smiled and gazed up towards the stars.

'But that is not the strangest part of the story,' he said. 'For this man had a special cap made, with a little hole in the back, so that he could see even when his head was covered – as it must always be in Ireland, for there are to be found small hawks, no bigger than a child's hand, which settle on a man's head and pluck out his hairs and take them to a wizard who lives under the rock of Killymaguish. There the hairs are made into magic potions, and no man whose hair has been so used can ever call his soul his own again.'

The point of the curved sword began to waver. The man

said in a slightly less angry voice, 'Yes, that is interesting. We have a story which is similar to that, in Byzantium.'

Grummoch said, 'I will break off my tale to hear yours, friend, for I am a simple man who delights in hearing good tales. Perhaps when I have heard yours, I shall be able to take it back to my chieftain in Ireland and gain the hand of his fairest daughter for telling it.'

He began to laugh then, as though the plan appealed to him. The man with the sword smiled at the simplicity of this great giant and then, with a shrug, said, 'The difference between our stories is that the hawks are very big ones.'

'How big?' asked Grummoch, putting his hands behind his broad back and rocking on his feet as he gazed up at the stars.

'About as broad in the wingspan as this,' said the guardian, stretching out his hands, the lantern in one, the sword in the other.

Grummoch's right foot shot out and the man fell on to his back. The sword clattered away into the dusk. The lantern rolled over the paving-stones, sending out a whirligig of light across the courtyard. Grummoch sat on the man, gently but firmly.

'I should have known better than to trust a foreigner,' said the guardian of the Imperial treasure house, sadly.

Grummoch said, 'If you are quiet and do not wriggle so much, I shall not hurt you at all. But if you as much as raise a whisper, I shall leave no more of you intact than would feed a sickly sparrow.'

The man said, 'That is understood, my friend. I am a fatalist. Only I would be grateful if you would sit on another part of me; I have always had a weak chest, and your weight brings on my old cough, which I thought this dry summer had almost cured.'

'With pleasure,' said Grummoch, as he moved lower down. But the guardian groaned so much at this, that Grummoch took off the man's belt and tied his ankles together. Then he tore the man's robe into strips and tied and gagged him.

'You understand, comrade,' he said, 'I could do much more, but I prefer to do less.'

The man nodded, for really he was a reasonable fellow and loved Irene no more than any other man. So Grummoch was able to join Harald, who was by this time down in the treasure cellar, stuffing goblets, plate, and bracelets into a sack which he had found on the floor.

Grummoch brought down the lantern, and when he flashed its beam round the place almost fell back with wonder.

'This is more than I ever dreamed of,' he said, 'and in my time I was not unused to such sights!'

When they had filled the sack, they clambered back up the stairs.

Their surprise did not come until they had passed back down the narrow alleyway and into the street again. Then they saw a sight which almost sent them scuttling back to the courtyard they had left. A mob of over fifty strong was waiting in the square, looking to right and left, waving swords and torches.

Grummoch went first into the street with the treasure sack on his back. The mob saw him and instantly a great howl went up.

'There they are ! There are the two who attacked us outside the Palace !' shouted a tall man with a pointed black cap. 'After them, friends ! Every blow we strike is a blow against Irene !'

At the end of the street they were in, Harald gasped, 'I cannot go much farther, Grummoch, I have a terrible stitch !'

The savage pattering of sandalled feet sounded behind them, the fierce shouts grew nearer. Stones began to rattle on the walls beside them.

Grummoch grunted hoarsely, 'The deer that cannot run gets eaten !'

Harald gasped out, 'Into that archway, friend. If we stay on the street they will catch us !'

In a moment they had turned into a curved archway. Grummoch swung the heavy door to behind him. They raced along a passage way, across a stone courtyard and then clambered over a wall. They fell straightway into a sloping meadow, where a stream flowed down towards a conduit. The place was surrounded by tall houses with many black windows, but it was night time and they rolled unashamedly down the slope. At last, standing knee-deep in the covered water-way, they dared to breathe again.

Above them the sounds of pursuit died away, and finally all was still again.

Grummoch said, 'Now let us try to make our way out of this city of evil. I saw a path beyond the conduit when the moon came out last; it leads to a gateway at the bottom end of this field.'

They began to walk slowly along the path, which

now shone grey in the moonlight. Just before they reached the broad gateway, Grummoch started back. There was something white, perched on the ledge beside the lintels, and the sound it made was not one which either of these men had heard before.

Then Harald burst out laughing at their fear. He moved forward to the white thing and took it up.

'Look,' he said, 'it is nothing but a baby, wrapped in a shawl.'

'And a very young baby at that,' said Grummoch, taking the little creature gently in his big hands and looking down at it. 'I have not seen one as young as this before. What a strange sound they make, my friend.'

Harald stumbled over something in the darkness of the wall. He bent down and then stood upright again with a sigh.

'The child's mother lies there. She is very young. It is sad that plague should be so cruel. She must have placed her baby there for safety before she fell.'

But Grummoch did not seem to hear him; the giant was so occupied with his tiny burden, trying not to jolt the baby, crooking it in the great angle of his arm so as to protect it.

'You must take the treasure sack now, comrade,' he said to Harald. 'I will carry this most precious piece of treasure.'

They went through the gateway and out into a rutted lane, edged with buildings of a more rustic character, as though they belonged to the outermost suburbs of the city.

Behind them, the clustered houses on the hill were illumined in the sullen glow of the many fires which now seemed to rage unchecked within Byzantium. Grummoch nodded back towards them and said, 'I am glad that we are away from that place, Harald. It was no sort of home for men like us.'

Harald answered, 'All the same, friend, we have not done badly. We have come away richer than we were when we first arrived there.'

Grummoch nodded as he shambled on along the uneven path in the dimness of the moonlight.

'Yes,' he said, 'and we have the baby as well. I always wanted a little baby to look after, Harald. It is strange, is it not? Now I remember that when I was a boy, my mother used to set me to look after our youngest child, Caedmac. It was very pleasant in the sunshine to swing him up and down and to listen to his laughter. He was a merry boy, was little Caedmac. I missed him when they sent me away from the village. Now we have a baby of our own.'

Harald did not know how to tell the giant that it would be almost as cruel for them to keep the baby as to leave it in the plague-ridden city; for they did not know where they might find themselves, what dangers they might meet; nor, most important of all, did either of them know how such a small child should be fed.

But the problem was solved for them quite simply. By dawn they walked into a narrow lane, bordered on either side by stunted shrubs and brown rustling reeds, and there they came upon a low hovel, built of wattle-and-daub, with a rushlight burning in the little window. Somewhere in the distance a dog barked at the sky, mournfully and without hope.

Now the baby began to wail again, as though it were desperately hungry. Grummoch looked helplessly at Harald and whispered, 'Perhaps if the Gods are with us, we might find milk for the bairn at this cottage.'

Harald nodded. 'It is worth risking,' he said, 'for we cannot walk much farther with it in this cold morning air. It must be chilled to the marrow, poor creature, as it is.'

Harald went forward and pushed at the cottage door gently, not wishing to frighten whoever might be therein. Yet, as a precaution, he held the hilt of his sword in readiness.

The sight which met his eyes caused him to forget all thoughts of combat, for this was the home of a quiet and gentle-spoken old couple, country folk, unlike the treacherous town-dwellers they had recently become accustomed to, during their weeks in Miklagard.

The white-haired old man was seated at a table, knotting together the strands of a broken fishing-net; the old lady sat at the fireside, stirring the contents of a small cauldron which bubbled on the fire and singing quietly as she stirred. In a far corner of the warm room, a young man was busy packing a small sack with provisions.

The three looked up in surprise as Harald entered, followed by Grummoch, who for the moment kept the baby concealed beneath his cloak.

At last the young man said uncertainly, 'Who are you?

What do you want at this hour? We are peaceful folk in this house. What do you want?'

Harald answered them in the Byzantine dialect which he had picked up during his stay in the Palace.

'We are travellers who would ask only that you give this baby something to keep it alive; and then, if you have anything to spare, we would be grateful for a mouthful of that porridge which you stir in the pot, lady, and a draught of milk to wash it down.'

He fumbled in the treasure sack and drew out a small silver bracelet set with garnets. This he held out towards the old lady; but she rose with such a look of disdain that the viking withdrew his offering in some shame.

She went forward and took the child from Grummoch and crooned to it and took it beside the fire, rocking it and whispering strange little words to it, until it too began to croon back, contentedly.

The old man put down his broken nets and said simply, 'We lost our first boy when he was of such an age. Always my wife has said that the good God would send him back to her; and now she thinks that her dream has come to pass.'

Grummoch gazed at him, wondering.

The young man stood up straight and said, 'You see, strangers, my aunt has dreamt the same dream three times, that men in armour like Gods, and one of them a giant, would come to our cottage one day and would bring back the child which was lost. You are her dream come to life. If you took the child away again, it would break her heart.'

Harald said, 'We shall not break her heart, young man.

The child is hers, for its mother is dead and we are not the sort of men to tend such a little one. Lady, the child is yours.'

The old woman gazed up at him speechlessly, but her eyes were wet with tears. Then she began to sing softly to the baby and the old man poured out two dishes of thick gruel for the travellers.

As they ate it, the young man said, 'Where do you travel, lords?'

And Grummoch answered, 'One place is as good as another, for men like us. Where do you suggest, young one?'

The young man grinned and replied, 'I go to join a trading ship, which sails northwards over the Inland Sea to do business with the Khazars. If you fancy such a voyage, I can speak to the captain, who is a good enough fellow, for a Bulgar.'

A little later, the three men left the cottage, where the old woman still wept with joy at the gift which the Gods of her dream had brought out of the dawn. The old man stood at the doorway, calling blessings after them. Harald ran back and pushed the silver bracelet into his hand.

'Keep this for the young child,' he said. 'It may buy him a sword one day.'

The old man gazed at him in wonder. 'A sword?' he said, almost fearfully, 'But what does the child want with a sword? A child wants other things, lord, before he comes to swords. And pray God this one never comes to swords and such like.'

There was nothing Harald could think of in reply to

this, for in the northern world the son of a chieftain was always given a sword as soon as he could walk.

Harald shook the old man by the hand and ran after his companions. They walked for a mile down a sunken and rutted lane, which at last opened out to show them the wide marshes surrounding the great Inland Sea. And as the morning broke fully, they came to a jetty where a long ship lay, its red sail already bellying in the strong breeze.

So Harald and Grummoch came to set course again for the north, leaning over the low gunwales and watching the smoking city of Miklagard slowly falling away behind them as the wind freshened.

After a while, Grummoch said to Harald, 'I think you had better wrap my cloak about those golden trinkets in the sack to stop them rattling. The captain of this ship may be a good fellow, for a Bulgar, but his eyes had a strange glint when he heard the sound the sack made as you set it on the deck. I do not trust him too far.'

Harald nodded. 'Nor do I,' he said.

Part Four

Late summer turned to autumn, and the days which followed seemed like a long dream to the two travellers. Sometimes it was a gay dream, as when they all gathered on the half deck of the trading ship and sang songs, or told impossible stories, at which Grummoch excelled. At other times it was a frightening dream, as when Harald woke with a start one night to find a dark figure bending over the treasure sack, trying to untie the hide thong with which it was fastened. When the viking moved, the man ran off into the darkness at the far end of the ship and Harald did not think it wise to follow him. He did not know which of the crew it might be, though the captain, Pazak, gave him a strange look the following morning, as though he wondered whether Harald suspected anyone in particular.

Yet for the most part, it was a fair enough voyage; the wind held, they put in at friendly villages on the shore of the Inland Sea and got good treatment from the Bulgars there, and never ran short of fresh food and good milk – though sometimes it was the milk of mares and not of cows or goats, and that took some getting used to.

One evening, Harald stood in the prow of the ship and said to Grummoch, 'Look, straight ahead lies our port, at the mouth of the big river, the Dnieper. I am now anxious to get back to my village by the fjord with this treasure, for I have been away for over a year and soon the winter will be on us, and travelling will be bad.'

Grummoch said, 'Why are you saying this now? What is in your mind, friend Harald? You are a crafty one and seldom speak without some good reason.'

Harald looked behind him before he answered, to see that no one overheard his words. Then he whispered, 'It has come to my mind that when we land at the mouth of the big river, we may find ourselves no longer free men; then Pazak will have gained both ways, by taking our treasure *and* by selling us as slaves. I have no wish to spend the winter so far from my village.'

Grummoch thought for a while and then said, 'You are right. Pazak accepted the few coins we offered him, for our passage, without any argument, and that is a bad sign in a sea-captain. They usually ask for twice as much as one offers. Now why should Pazak be so meek? Only because he thinks to gain in the end. Yes, you are right, Harald. So what shall we do, then?'

Harald whispered to him again, and the giant nodded his great head in agreement, smiling broadly all the time.

So it was that in the night, when the ship lay less than a mile off the river mouth, Harald and Grummoch slipped over the side with their treasure and pushed off in the small landing-raft which was towed at the stern. No one saw them go and though they found it hard work to send the raft through the water with the two boards which they took with them, by dawn they ran to the salt-marsh flats beside the mouth of the Dnieper, and waded up to the hard ground above.

When the sun had gained its strength and warmed

them again, they set off northwards, keeping the broad river in sight on their right hand. Beyond the great river stretched an open land, still green with summer, but vast and empty. Though once when they were walking on a little ridge that ran northwards, they looked down and saw a long line of horsemen making their way beside the river, in the direction of the Inland Sea.

Grummoch shaded his eyes and gazed at them. 'I have seen men like that before, my friend,' he said. 'They are Khazars, riding to meet the trading ship and to buy slaves, no doubt, as well as the wine and fruits Pazak was bringing from Miklagard.'

Harald stared in the direction of the horsemen. They wore high fur caps and carried long lances. They sat slackly on their ponies, like men who almost lived in the saddle, moving with every movement of their steeds.

Harald said, 'I understand the respect in your voice when you mention the Khazars now, Grummoch. They seem a formidable folk.'

Grummoch nodded and smiled grimly. 'Yes, my friend, they are,' he said. 'Come, let us strike northwards as fast as we can; if they were to see us, they might well swim their horses across the river to come up here after us. They are a curious people, and like to know what strangers are doing in their country.'

But the Khazars did not seem to notice them, and at the end of the day they came to a small village of skin huts, set in a little hollow. Dogs ran at them, barking, but an old man with long white hair rose from beside a fire and called the animals away. Then he came forward to meet the two, holding his hand to his forehead as a sign of peace. Grummoch, who had picked up more than a smattering of Bulgar and Khazar dialects when he had been a slave among them, spoke to him, asking for shelter and food. The old man led them courteously to his skin tent and gave them bread and meat and mare's milk. In the morning as they left, he refused to accept any payment for his hospitality, and even sent two of his sons to guide the travellers northwards for some miles, so that they should not lose their way in the marshes which spread out on either side of the great river, from place to place.

These young men said little, but smiled a great deal, and when they had parted, Harald said, 'I do not trust men who smile as much as that, friend Grummoch. I suspect that they may well ride to tell the Khazars where we are. What do you think?'

Grummoch said, 'It would be no unusual thing if they did, I suppose. Perhaps it would be wise if we were to move away from the river, and try to find ourselves horses somewhere. Great herds of them graze on the plains a little farther to the north.'

They left the river then and for three days looked for a horse. But it seemed that these creatures had moved to other grazing grounds, for the travellers saw very few of them, and those few were so sensitive of sight and hearing that it was impossible to get near enough to them to catch one. So when the food which they had brought away from the skin village was exhausted, the two men decided that they must go back to the river, where at least they might be fortunate enough to kill wild fowl and so keep themselves from starving.

One morning, Harald sat down on the river bank and began to laugh. Grummoch stared at him in concern, wondering whether he had lost his reason with hunger. But Harald shook his head and said, 'No, my friend, I am not mad – only very sane, so sane that I think what fools we are to strike off into this empty land with no more provisions than a bag of treasure! What if we throw the treasure into the river and turn our steps southwards again? We should travel lighter and might even be lucky enough to get a ship to take us back to Miklagard. Perhaps things are better there now. At least, there is food to eat there.'

Grummoch was about to agree with him, when round the bend of the river came a long, heavily-laden rowing boat, propelled by six oars. At first the two men thought of running away, but then Harald said, 'Let us wait and see if they mean well; we can always run when we have decided that.'

When the boat drew level with them, a man in a bright steel helmet called to them, 'We are Bulgars, trading in Kiev. We are short of two oarsmen. Will you come with us, friends?'

Grummoch said, 'I have often heard of Kiev. It seems to be a growing town and I would much like to see it. Shall we go with them?'

Harald nodded and said, 'I would go almost anywhere, rather than walk another day across this empty land. It fills my dreams every night. I feel that I shall never see a town again! Let us go with them, by all means.'

They waded out and were picked up. As they boarded the boat, they were careful not to let their treasure sack rattle this time. They were also careful not to let its weight be seen by the rowers who helped them into the boat, but pretended that the sack contained their cloaks and heavy winter jackets.

So they became oarsmen in the Bulgar boat, sitting next to each other on the same bench. The merchant, who had hailed them, was a kindly man, and made no secret of the fact that he was glad to have two such strong fellows in his boat. He fed them well and offered them a place at the oars on the return trip, but Grummoch smilingly refused, saying, 'I have news that my grandmother in Orkney is anxious to talk to me. You see, she sent me on an errand to a neighbour in Ireland ten years ago, to borrow a dozen eggs that she needed, to make a pudding for my uncle, who is in bed with a bad Caledonian cold. I am afraid I was a bad lad, and forgot about the pudding, and now my uncle is getting restive. So I must go back and tell my grandmother, in Iceland, that her neighbour in Ireland had stopped keeping hens.'

The merchant stared at Grummoch, whose face was deadly serious.

'I do not understand,' he said. 'You said your grandmother was in Orkney, and now you say that she is in Iceland.'

Grummoch nodded. 'Yes,' he said. 'That is so. My family move about so quickly that it does not do to be too long away from them. That is why I am anxious to get back as soon as I can. Otherwise, who knows, grandmother might have run all the way to Miklagard with her rheumatics to look for me.'

The merchant shook his head and walked away from

Grummoch. After that, he did not invite them to sail with him on the return trip.

But they did not see Kiev. On the eighth day of rowing against the sluggish stream, the merchant allowed them to pull in to the shore to rest and to light fires, for a cold wind had sprung up across the great plains and chilled the oarsmen to the bone.

Some of the men sat about on the shore, while others wandered here and there, looking for anything that would burn. Grummoch and Harald, carrying their sack, as they always did, walked away from the others, to a stretch of low and stunted scrub which they thought they might uproot for fuel. But the work was hard and after a while they sat down, rubbing their chafed hands and wondering whether it was worth while risking the edges of their swords in trying to cut the tough branches.

It was when they were talking of this that they heard sudden shrill cries from the direction of the river. At first they paid little attention to these shouts, thinking that some of the men were playing a game to keep themselves warm. But when they heard the merchant's voice hallooing, they stood up, to look over the scrub and to see what was the matter. They saw two sights which gave them a start; first, they saw that the boat was pulling out as fast as it could go into midstream, and secondly they saw that the hillside above them was lined with men on ponies, men wearing high skin caps and carrying long lances.

Grummoch spread his chafed hands out and said, 'What will be, will be ! So that was why they were shouting – they wanted us to get back into the boat.'

But Harald did not answer. He felt too disheartened

now to speak. The two men put their swords back into their scabbards, realizing that they could not fight against such odds, and waited for the horsemen to come down the slope and capture them. But for a while nothing happened, and at last Harald said, 'Come on, let us walk along the river again. Perhaps they mean us no harm.'

Grummoch merely grunted and shouldered the sack once more. Then they set off walking and, as they did so, the men on horses kicked their mounts forward and rode alongside them, along the crown of the ridge. When the two friends stopped, so did the Khazars; when they walked on quickly, the Khazars spurred on their ponies to a faster speed.

Grummoch said, 'They are playing with us, shepherding us to their village. I wish I felt strong enough to leap into the river and try swimming across.'

Harald answered, 'That would do no good. Their horses can no doubt swim better than we can, besides, we should be weighed down by the treasure.'

At last they topped a hill and saw below them a sprawling settlement of skin tents, wagons, and thorn fences. Many fires burned there and horses, cows, and dogs seemed to wander wherever they wished, undisturbed by the swarms of children. From the village came up a babble of voices, shouting, laughter, singing, which was made more confusing by the barking of dogs, the lowing of oxen, and the high whinnying of horses.

Harald drew his hand across his brows and said, 'I am not going down there, into that hullabaloo!' He sat down, but did not stay long on the ground, for a horseman suddenly rode up behind him and urged him forward with the butt-end of his long lance. Harald rose again ruefully and went down the slope with Grummoch, between the hordes of shouting children and the grazing cattle.

Now the silent horsemen began to shout and laugh. swinging their ponies up and round, and then suddenly galloping off furiously to make a circuit of the settlement, throwing their long lances into the air and catching them as they rode. The children shouted out their applause and the dogs barked as though everything was immensely exciting.

Then the leader of the horsemen prodded the two friends forward towards a big tent of goat's hair and when they were before the open door, jumped from his pony and pushed them inside.

An old man sat on a pile of cushions and sheepskins in the centre of the tent, warming his hands by a smouldering cowdung fire. He was surrounded by small children and dogs, which rolled about on the carpeted floor of the tent happily together, pretending to fight each other, nibbling, wrestling, while the old man surveyed them gently, quietly amused at their antics.

When the two friends stood before him, however, he waved the children away to the back of the tent, and shooed the dogs after them. Only then did he raise his heavy-lidded eyes and look up at Harald and Grummoch. They saw that his face was incredibly wrinkled and old-looking. His long white moustaches reached almost to his chest and he wore great gold rings in his ears. Beneath his sleeveless jacket of white sheepskin he had on a long robe of heavy red silk stained down the front with wine spots and grease. His fingers, though laden with dull-glinting gold rings, were dirty and their nails cracked and horny.

He surveyed them in silence for a while, smiling mysteriously, and then he said in perfect Norse, 'I began to think that my men had lost you. They rode the length of the great river again and again after they had heard about you from the two sons of old Kazan. But sooner or later in this land one finds what one seeks. So they found you at last. And now you can put your treasure sack on the floor. It seems a very heavy burden and there is no need for you to carry it any farther. I shall look after it for you.'

Grummoch put the sack down, staring wide-eyed at this strange old man. Harald said, 'How is it, old one, that you speak like a man of the fjords?'

The old man said, 'First, I must ask you not to call me "old one" in front of the children, for here it is a rude term of address. I do not want them to pick up bad habits, for they are my grandchildren and must grow up to address me properly. You must call me "King of the Marshland". As for your question, viking, it is very easy to answer. I have been in many strange parts in my time, and once spent five years in the north myself, seeking my fortune with the men of Sven Red-eye. But that is all past; I brought back a wife from your folk and she taught me much of your tongue, before, alas, she died. Then later I was lucky enough to buy a slave from some Wends who came this way, trying to get to Miklagard overland. He was a Christian priest and helped me a great deal in the writing of runes, among other things. He died only last year, from over-eating when we had our Spring festival. I was sorry to lose him, for he had a most amusing store of tales to tell.'

Harald said, 'You are a courteous man, King of the Marshland; why then do you take our treasure – for I will not try to deceive you as to the contents of that sack?'

The old King nodded slyly and said, 'It would be better not to try to deceive me about anything at all, for I have long ears and sharp eyes, in spite of my age. But I will answer you : I take your treasure sack to keep it safely for you until you return. You see, I mean you no harm. I intend to send you back to your own land, and I ask in return that you should bring a hundred or two of the men from the fjords down here next year, when the rivers have thrown off their winter ice. When you do that, I shall return your treasure to you – but only then. Is that understood?'

Grummoch said, 'What do you want vikings for, King of the Marshland? Haven't you men of your own?'

The old man nodded and said, 'Yes, I have many men, but they are not good as foot-soldiers. Take their ponies from them and they are useless – why, they can hardly walk, my friend, and the task I wish to accomplish needs men who can fight on foot or on horseback.'

Harald said, 'What do you wish to do, King of the Marshland?'

The old man felt inside his red robe and took out a small ivory ball from an inner pocket. This he flung into the air, without watching where it went, and caught it at the side, behind his back, above his head, anywhere, all the time staring into Harald's eyes. At last, when he was tired of playing with the ball, he said, 'I intend to capture the city of Kiev and to become the greatest King that the plains have ever known. And afterwards, I intend to make war on the Franks first, and on the Roman Emperor second. When I have done that, I shall go perhaps to Spain and rule over our Muslim brothers there.'

Harald gasped at the old man's dream of power, but he found wit enough to ask ironically, 'And the north? Will you not conquer the north while you are about it?'

The old man's lips twisted in a sardonic smile and he

answered the viking in the same tone which Harald had used.

'No,' he said, 'I shall spare the north, provided that you come back in the Spring with two hundred berserks and help me on the first stage of my journey.'

Harald bowed before him, with sarcasm, then, and said, 'Very well, King of the Marshland. What will be, will be. We will leave our treasure because we must, and we will go home to the north.'

The old man smiled and said, 'You are a sensible young fellow for a viking, I must say. I shall send you north on good horses, with a strong escort. We shall have to see to that very soon, for in a month the rivers will be ice-bound. So I shall see that you are taken beyond the great portage, and put on a longship there.'

Harald gasped at the old man's confidence. 'A longship', he said. 'How do you know of a longship so far away?'

The old man closed his eyes and rocked beside the fire with amusement at the viking's tone of wonder.

'With fast riders like mine, I can keep in touch with most things which happen on the Plains, my friend. There is nothing magic about it. The villagers at the Great Portage are already waiting for Haakon Baconfat to come trading with them before the winter starts. He will take you home, I have no doubt, if you tell him I say he must.'

Harald sat down on the ground with sheer shock then. 'Why,' he said, 'I have known Haakon Baconfat since I was a lad of twelve. He used to make wooden swords for me and teach me to track bears.'

The old man nodded and said, 'Yes, he is a good man

with children. It was his sister I married, you know. So in a way, we are relatives.'

Thereafter, Harald felt that nothing in the world would surprise him. He lay back on the cushions beside the cow-dung fire and ate the good meal which a Khazar woman brought for them. Then he drank deeply of the strong barley beer which the old King poured out of a bulging skin-bottle. And then he fell fast asleep, too tired and well-fed to bother about anything – even about losing the treasure.

And in the morning, he and Grummoch sat astride two sturdy Khazar ponies, wearing sheepskin jackets and high fur hats, just like their escort. The old King came to the doorway of his black tent and waved them on their journey, saying, 'Go lightly and easily, and come back in the Spring – if you ever want to see the contents of your treasure sack again !'

Grummoch, whose feet hung down to the ground, made such a wry grimace at the old man's words, that all the horsemen shouted with laughter. Then, as the autumnal sun struck across the broad grassland to their right hands, the party set off northwards, skirting Kiev lest they might be ambushed.

Old Thorn, the headman of the village by the fjord, sat outside his wooden house in the early winter sunshine, wrapped in his thickest cloak and staring across the cold green water. His old dog, Thorri, snuggled beside him, turning up grateful eyes to his master, who scratched the dog's ear thoughtfully.

Thorn was thinking about the shipload of men who had sailed away from the village over a year and a half before.

'Rascals, the whole lot of them!' he said bad-temperedly to the dog. 'Enjoying themselves in Ireland, no doubt. Living off the fat of the land while we of the village scrape to make ends meet, and winter coming on as well.'

The dog seemed to understand what Thorn was saying, for he put on a sorrowful expression, and lay down with a sigh at the old headman's feet.

'Never mention Harald Sigurdson to me again,' said Thorn, as though addressing the dog. Thorri the dog looked up with wide old eyes as though he meant to say that he would never mention that wicked Harald again.

Thorn's youngest daughter, little Asa, called him in to eat his breakfast. The old man grumbled and began to rise from his bench, clutching his blackthorn stick tightly.

Just then two men came down the hill above the village, one a man of a normal size, the other as big as a man and half a man. Both were heavily bearded and wore tall fur caps.

Old Thorn stared up at them in surprise, wondering who they might be. Then he called into the room, 'Keep an eye on the pigs at the back of the house, Little Asa. Two strangers come; they may be thieves.'

But the two men did not turn aside to snatch up a pig from behind the little house. Instead they came up to Thorn and the smaller of the men took the headman by the hand and said, 'Greetings, old man! How are you these days?'

Thorn was about to make some sharp reply when he saw the face of the man who spoke, and recognized it, despite the high fur cap and the thick golden beard.

'Why, Harald Sigurdson!' he said. 'Where have you been, you rogue? Where are the others? Where is the good ship we gave you? And who is this great hulking giant?'

Harald laughed at the spate of questions and answered, 'All in good time, Thorn.' Then he called inside the house, 'Little Asa, lay a good meal for us. We have walked for three days through the forest and are hungry! If we hadn't found berries to eat, we should surely have starved to death!'

Little Asa came out and almost fell back in a faint to see the giant Grummoch, who looked an amazingly hairy fellow what with his beard and his thick sheepskin coat and fur cap. But she soon recovered and led them inside, laughing and crying at the same time.

So, over a good meal and a draught of mead, Harald told his story – some of it sad, some of it happy. Until he came to the old King of the Marshland.

At this part of the tale, Thorn rose from his seat and thumped his hand on the oak table-top. 'What!' he stormed, 'after all that, to lose the treasure to that old heathen! I will have you whipped, both of you, for foolish fellows, wastrels and rogues! I will call the villagers together right now and have it done!'

But Harald shouted to him to sit down, and then, from an inner pocket in his sheepskin jacket, he took out a deerskin bag, bulging so tightly that it was almost round. Slowly he untied the hide-thong about the neck of the bag and then let fall onto the table a stream of precious stones, of all colours and sizes, until they rolled about the oaken board and even onto the floor. Thorn's eyes almost came out of his head.

'But you said you had lost the treasure!' he said. 'Why, there is enough wealth here for every man of this village to live a life of ease, with ships a-plenty!'

Harald grinned up at him and said, 'When one is among crafty folk, one must stay awake all night. That is what I did, one night, and with my knife prised the stones out of all the gold and silver goblets in the treasure sack. The old King of the Marshland has not nearly so good a bargain as he thought!'

Thorn sat back in his seat, gasping with amazement.

'Well,' he said, 'this is a gift from Odin himself! We must divide this treasure up, so that every man of this village may have his deserts.'

Harald said quietly, 'And we must set one share aside for Haro, who is certain to turn up again, like a bad coin, you can be bound!'

It was at this point that little Asa said shyly, 'I do not

think so, Harald. A sea-faring man passed this way a week ago with a wonderful tale of a viking who had gone to Jebel Tarik and married there a Princess called Marriba. I did not dare tell father at the time. I think that Haro has his treasure safely enough where he is.' And no one disagreed with her.

Then suddenly little Asa said with a smile, 'But what are we to do with this great giant here? He will surely eat us out of house and home! Why on earth did you bring such a one back here with you, Harald?'

Harald laughed aloud at the expression on Grummoch's broad face. He looked like a little boy who has suddenly been scolded for something which he thought was long forgotten.

But Harald came to his rescue and said, 'Have no fear, little Asa; he will be worth his weight, which is considerable, in gold. You will see that I am right. He is the most wonderful nurse for small babies that ever you saw. Aren't you, Grummoch?'

The giant hung his head and mumbled shamefacedly.

Little Asa rose and patted him on the shoulder as she made her way to the door.

'That is great news,' she said with a smile, 'for all the mothers of our village are beside themselves with extra work in this season, for as you know it is the time when we salt the meat for winter storing. They will be delighted to have such a playmate for their little ones.'

Then she leaned out of the door and began to call, 'Little Sven! Gnorre! Haakon! Knud! Elsa! Come, all of you, quickly! I have a lovely giant for you to play with!

Come quickly before he magics himself away with fright !
Come on, all of you !'

Grummoch twisted his great hands and said, 'Now I
wish I had stayed in Miklagard. At least I had a sword to
defend myself with there.'

But Harald said gently, 'Do not worry, friend, our children are kind ones. They will not hurt you.'

Then they all laughed. And such was the manner of
the homecoming of Harald Sigurdson.

If you have enjoyed this book and would like
to know about others which we publish,
why not join the Puffin Club? You will
receive the club magazine, *Puffin Post*, four
times a year and a smart badge and
membership book. You will also be able to
enter all the competitions. For details of cost
and an application form, send a stamped addressed
envelope to:

The Puffin Club Dept. A
Penguin Books Limited
Bath Road
Harmondsworth
Middlesex